NIV VERSUS THE KJV

A CRITIQUE OF THE NIV BIBLE AND
A DEFENSE OF THE KJV BIBLE

Dennis H. Helton

DEDICATION

I DEDICATE THIS BOOK TO ALL WHO BELIEVE IN THE PRESERVED WORDS OF GOD.

Psalm 12:7 *Thou shalt keep them, O LORD, thou shalt **preserve** them from this generation **for ever**. 8 The wicked walk on every side, when the vilest men are exalted.*

TABLE OF CONTENTS

QUESTIONS ANSWERED IN THIS BOOK

- **How Many Bible Texts Did God Write?**
- **What Are The Underlying Texts Of The NIV And KJV Bibles?**
- **Does The NIV Text Differ From The KJV Text?**
- **What Do NIV Editors And Apologists Say?**
- **Is The Divinity Of Christ Both Proven And Discredited By The NIV?**
- **Is 'Word Translation' The Same As 'Thought Translation?'**
- **What Advantage Is The 'Ye' And 'Thee' In The KJV?**
- **Is The NIV Version Easier To Read Than The KJV Translation?**
- **Why Do Most People Buy The NIV?**
- **Did God Preserve Copies Of The Original Manuscripts?**
- **Where Is God's Preserved Word Today?**
- **Are The Original Bible Manuscripts The Only Ones Inerrant?**
- **Why Are 'King James Only' Advocates Labeled 'Ruckmanites?'**
- **Do Some Bible Fundamentalists Hold Similar Views To Liberals?**
- **Who Is The "Morning Star," Jesus Or Lucifer?**

- **What Was Common About A Shrine Prostitute And A Sodomite?**
- **What Do Critics Of The King James Bible Mutually Claim Against It?**
- **Was Mary, The Mother Of Jesus, Without Sin?**
- **Who Are The Promoters Of New Age Bibles And What Are Their Motives?**
- **Is Scholarship Essential For Selecting The Right Bible?**
- **Can A Bible With 17 Missing Verses Be Trusted?**
- **Who Are The True Traditional Bible Fundamentalists?**

INTRODUCTION

Why this writing?

The purpose of this writing is not to judge the hearts or the motives of NIV Bible users; however, this paper is presented to those who are open-minded to facts. If the reader has a closed mind or is biased in favor of New Age bibles, do not waste your time reading this material. If the reader is a seeker of truth, continue reading. Someone has well said, There is none so blind as those who refuse to see.

The Scriptures teach the following principles of seeking truth:

> *Proverbs 18:13: He that answereth a matter before he heareth it, it is folly and shame unto him.*
>
> *Galatians 4:16: Am I therefore become your enemy, because I tell you the truth?*

CHAPTER 1

THE NEW AGE BIBLE TEXTS

In 1881, Brook F. Westcott (bishop of the Anglican church) and Fenton A. Hort (Anglican professor at Cambridge University) changed the traditional Greek text in 8,413 places using the corrupt Vaticanus and Sinaiticus manuscripts as the basis *(Which Bible Is God's Word,?* p.70).

• The Vaticanus and the Sinaiticus disagreed with each other over 3,000 times in the four Gospels alone *(Which Bible Is God's Word,* p.102). Westcott and Hort completely ignored the fact that Christian scholars of centuries past had consistently rejected the corrupt Vaticanus and Sinaiticus documents.

• Westcott, in a letter to the Archbishop of Canterbury March 4, 1890, said, "No one now, I suppose, holds that the first three chapters of Genesis, for example, give a literal history" *(Let's Weigh the Evidence,* p. 77).

• Westcott and Hort were instrumental in pioneering textual criticism. Their eclectic text (selected from various sources or variant readings) was promoted by Eberhard Nestle and Kurt Aland and is used in most fundamental Bible colleges and universities today. The text most commonly used at the time of this writing is the Nestle-Aland Greek New Testament - 26th Edition. (There is now a 27th edition of the Nestle-Aland Greek New Testament.)

• Eberhard Nestle's son, Erwin, said, "My father knew quite well that a certain one sidedness adhered to his text" *(New Age Bible Versions*, p. 496).

The Corrupted Westcott-Hort Text is the leaven that has leavened the whole lump of Christianity.

• The NIV (New International Version) is an interpretation of these revised Greek manuscripts.

Greek text of the NIV

Of the about 5,300 Greek texts existing in papyrus fragments, uncials, cursive and lectionaries, only 1 percent or less agree with the Greek text of the NIV.

• **Papyri:** Small pieces of papyrus; fragments made from papyrus plant. It is brittle. Most do not have many verses on them. Of 88 now, 13 (15%) agree with the Westcott-Hort text.

• **Uncial:** Greek manuscripts written in large inch-long (twelfth part) capital letters that run together. They are without accent, punctuation, and verse/chapter division. There are 267 uncials of which 9 (3%) agree with the Westcott-Hort text.

• **Cursive** (minuscule): Greek manuscripts written in longhand or cursive. Their letters flow together. There are 2,764 preserved today of which 23 (1%) agree with Westcott-Hort.

• **Lectionaries:** Portions of Scripture in Greek and Latin Bibles that were read in the churches on certain days. All 2,143 agree with the Received Text of our King James Bible.

2 Corinthians 2:17: For we are not as many, which corrupt the word of God: but as of sincerity, but as of God, in the sight of God speak we in Christ.

God has preserved His Words in the ben Chayyim OT Masoretic Hebrew and the NT Byzantine Greek. The King James Bible is a trustworthy translation of these manuscripts for English speaking people.

D.A. Waite says, "Of 5,255 manuscripts, 99.15% agree with the Received Text. Only 0.85% agrees with Westcott-Hort" - (*Four Reasons for Defending the King James Bible*, p.15). This is why our King James Bible has been referred to as the Majority Text Bible.

Westcott and Hort referred to the Majority Text of the King James Bible as a *Vile Text*. They also admired Charles Darwin, agreeing wholeheartedly with his atheistic theory of evolution - (Dick Cimino, *The Book*, and p.1 of the foreword).

The writer is thankful to God for Tabernacle Baptist College of Greenville, S.C. and a few other Christian schools for using the KJV (King James Version) which is a translation from the Masoretic Hebrew and the Byzantine Greek texts (Textus Receptus). Most Christian colleges use a Bible text based on the 1881 Westcott-Hort revision. Some schools are ambivalent in their Greek text preference. A fundamentalist Christian university in Greenville, S. C. uses only the King James Bible for preaching but uses the Westcott-Hort text in its Greek department (*Defending The King James Bible*, p. 218).

One faculty professor of this school staunchly defends the Westcott-Hort Greek Text in his booklet, *The Truth About The King James Version Controversy.* Instead of pointing out numerous errors of the Westcott-Hort Text, the professor devotes over half of his booklet to attacking the faults of Peter Ruckman and discrediting the King James Greek Text.

Dr. Stewart Custer says, "The Alexandrian text (presumably Vaticanus and Sinaiticus and perhaps Alexandrinus) is older and better attested than the others" *(The Truth About The King James Version,* p. 9: emphasis by the writer}. The writer does not agree. The Alexandrian texts may be older because they survived in time due to rejection and non-use by established orthodox Churches. It certainly is not better attested than the Byzantine text.

Dr. Custer also thinks that only the teaching is preserved (*The Truth About The King James Version,* pp. 12, 13). Try to fit *teaching* in Psalms 12:6; Isaiah 40:8; Matthew 24:35; Luke 4:4; I Peter 1:25.

Dr. Custer also prefers to disclaim the authority of I John 5:7 in the King James Bible. He gives his reason against the validity of I John 5:7 by saying, "In this context it distracts from the direction of thought that John manifested" (The Truth About The King James Version, p. 14). Dr. Custer also uses Scofield's note to support his argument (the Scofield Bible uses the King James translation). The absence of I John 5:7 matches quite well with the Bibles of Roman Catholicism and Jehovah Witness which are translations from the corrupted Alexandrian Greek manuscripts that were used by Westcott and Hort. Neither will you find I John 5:7 in most of the other New Age Bible versions that are translations (or *thought* interpretations) of the Westcott-Hort revision.

(**Note:** The Scofield Bible is a good reference Bible, but its notes are not without faults and errors. For example, on page 1,325, the center references "o" and "q" denies the validity of I John 5:7 and the "in earth" of I John 5:8. Other faulty notes are also found: page 1,353, center reference "e;" page 1,272, center reference "a;" page 1,175, footnote "1;" page 1,069, footnote "1.")

Other New Age Bibles:

The Revised Standard Version (**RSV**), The New American Version, The New American Standard Bible (**NASB**), The New English Bible (**NEB**), The New International Version (**NIV**), Contemporary English Version (**CEV**), Living Bible (**LB**), Todays English Version (**TEV**, or Good News For Modern Man), The New Testament in Modern English by J.B. Phillips, New King James, etc.

Kurt Aland believes that the Byzantine Text (of the King James) is a revision of a third century text. Other textual critics insist that the Majority Text repeatedly offers us variations with little or no claim to being original (*Which Bible?* pp. 33-35). These beliefs were propagated by the Tracterians of the Oxford Movement (higher critics) and are emulated by our modern-day Westcott-Hort fundamentalist brethren.

Our Westcott-Hort Fundamentalist brethren prefer to follow after Bible textual critics, such as Westcott, Hort,

Aland, Simon, Astruc, Geddes, Eichhorn, Semler, DeWette, Hollander, Kuenen, Ewald, Wellhausen, Griesbach, Mohler, Lachmann, Tregelles, Wiseman, Coleridge, Schleiermacher, Smith, Tischendorf, Souter, Newman, Schaff, Jerome, Ellicott, Lightfoot, Moulton, Stanley, Moffatt, Weymouth, Goodspeed, and others.

The Westcott-Hort Fundamentalist brethren do not choose to stand with those men who have defended the Traditional Text such as Tyndale, Beza, Geerlings, Colwell, Clark, Hoskier, Fuller, Sightler, Scrivener, Hills, Doughty, Wilson, Brown, Hodges, Coray, Willoughby, Martin, Wilkinson, Cook, Cartwright, Melanchthon, Beckett, Hemphill, Stringer, Waite, and many other reliable scholars. Also include all of the Reformers, many thousands of unknown dedicated Christians and unimportant Bible students such as this writer.

Psalms 11:3: If the foundations be destroyed, what can the righteous do?

The writer believes that an old axiom speaks volumes here; it says, *Birds of a feather flock together.* Obviously, we gravitate toward those with whom we agree with the most.

Which Bible text has the reader chosen? Has the reader investigated or just following the side that they believe more knowledgeable and spiritual? Which Bible has the reader chosen?

- Did God fail to preserve His Word in an accurate text for the common people?
- Should Christians wait around a few decades for a "better attested" text while the professors sort it all out?

Apparently, Dr. Custer and his associates believe that they have the superior text: his defense of the corrupt Westcott-Hort Text is well supported by his school's staff.

Questions arise:

- Why does Dr. Custer's school use the Westcott-Hort Text instead of the King James Greek Text in their Greek department?
- Does this school lack confidence in the traditional Byzantine Greek Text?
- Does this school believe that there are no significant differences between the Greek text of Westcott-Hort/Nestle'-Aland and that of the King James?
- Does the staff of this school believe that the Westcott-Hort Text is more accurate than the Byzantine Greek Text?
- If this school believes that the Westcott-Hort Text is more accurate, why don't they preach from an English translation of this revision such as the ASB, NASB or the RSV?

Many Westcott-Hort fundamentalists love to lump King James advocates together with Peter Ruckman. Apparently, this makes them feel comfortable in using the Westcott-Hort text. Strangely, they appear to be shy about openly defending the Westcott-Hort Text by name. Perhaps they are afraid of losing support from good people who do not know that they favor the corrupt Westcott-Hort Greek Text over the traditional King James Greek Text.

The writer has observed a common pattern of the Westcott-Hort fundamentalist brethren concerning both texts of the King James and Westcott-Hort:

• The Westcott-Hort "fundamentalists" will rarely, if ever, point to any errors of the Westcott-Hort text; instead, they will laud its alleged great qualities.

• The NIV promoters will begin by extolling the great scholarship of Westcott and Hort. (So what, scholarship is not the main prerequisite for handling God's Word.)

• Next, these Westcott-Hort "fundamentalists" will praise the Christian dedication and spiritual depth of Westcott and Hort. (The writer is convinced that they were no more than liberal apostates.)

• The Westcott-Hort brethren will name other fundamentalists, who have used the Westcott-Hort revision, as if this gave absolute veracity to its text.

• Our Westcott-Hort fundamentalist brethren will conclude their defense of the Westcott-Hort text by discrediting the King James text. They will exaggerate the least trivial fault of the King James and glowingly refer to its alleged errors.

Some of the Westcott-Hort fundamentalists exhibit poor doctrinal exposition as well as demonstrating an intolerant and mean spirit toward King James advocates.

For example:

• One Westcott-Hort professor in a fundamentalist school (Greenville, SC) expounds that Jesus made fermented wine at the marriage in Cana (John 2:1-11).

The cup (grape juice) in the New Testament is Jesus' blood (I Corinthians 11:25). Jesus' pure untainted blood cannot be symbolized with fermented (leavened) grape juice because leaven is a type of evil, hypocrisy, and false doctrine (Matthew 16:6, 11-12; Luke 12:1; I Corinthians 5:7-8).

The LORD'S Passover, which pictured the sacrificial Lamb of God (Exodus 12:1-14), was to be eaten with unleavened bread. Of course, Jesus is our Passover (I Corinthians 5:7; John 1:29). It is highly unlikely that fermented grape juice (leavened wine) would be used in the Lord's Supper since leaven was strictly forbidden in the Jewish household before the Passover and with the Passover itself. Leaven was even forbidden during the days of the Feast of Unleavened Bread that followed immediately after the Passover.

Question # 1: Would Jesus make fermented (leavened) wine, which is a type of evil, to symbolize His pure blood?

Answer: No.

Question # 2: Would Jesus put the bottle to His neighbor thereby making him drunk?

Answer: No.

The putting of the bottle to a man is the only way he can become a drunkard. This could very likely rob a man of his opportunity for salvation. If Jesus made fermented wine at the marriage supper of Cana, He would be going against the Scriptural teaching of Habakkuk and also the apostle Paul.

> *Habakkuh 2:15: Woe unto him that giveth his neighbour drink, that puttest thy bottle to him, and makest him drunken also, that thou mayest look on their nakedness!*

> *I Corinthians 6:10: Nor thieves nor covetous, nor drunkards, nor revilers, nor extortioners shall inherit the kingdom of God.*

Question # 3: Would Jesus be a stumbling block to the weak in the faith?

Answer: No.

The Scriptures teach against becoming a stumbling block to the weak and it is certain that Jesus, who would have all men to be saved, would not do so (Romans 14:13; I Corinthians 8:9; 2 Peter 3:9).

Question # 4: Would Jesus go against His Word?

Answer: No.

Jesus would not go against His Word that teaches that a man is not wise when he looks upon fermented wine.

> *"...For thou hast magnified thy Word above all thy name (Psalms 138:2b).*

> *Proverbs 20:1: Wine is a mocker, strong drink is raging: and whosoever is deceived thereby is not wise. See also Proverbs 23:31-32.*

The writer does not have to wrestle over the answers to these questions. No lost drunkard will be able to point a finger at Jesus at the White Throne Judgment and accuse Him of contributing to his demise.

Apparently, the Westcott-Hort "fundamentalist" university professor that believes that Jesus made fermented wine does not believe that Jesus is wise.

• Another Westcott-Hort professor in a fundamentalist school (Greenville, SC) caused a student to be expelled from that school because the student refused to apologize for his belief in the King James Bible as an accurate and trustworthy translation of God's Word in English.

The student (a candidate for a master's degree) was also laughed at by some of the classroom students, as well as ridiculed by the professor who caused his expulsion. When the humiliated student appealed to the president of that school (in writing), the president sidestepped the issue and avoided a categorical answer to the student. The school president appeared delighted in reprimanding the student for refusing to buckle-under to the Westcott-Hort professor, implying that the student was rude. The school president sided with the teacher against the King James Bible preference. This story was directly related to the writer by the student who was soon afterwards expelled. The writer also read both letters, the student's letter to the president and the president's reply to the student.

So much for the endorsement of some fundamentalists!

The writer heard the president of this same fundamentalist school state over a radio broadcast that he used the King James Bible for preaching only because it was the Standard Bible of the people and because it had a certain poetical beauty to it. The writer does not believe that these two reasons alone are sufficient to justify using the King James Bible. The King James Bible is either a trustworthy and true translation from the preserved Hebrew and Greek texts, or it is not. You either believe "it all" or you do not believe it "at all." Actually, the statement by that school leader implies that the KJV is lacking in accuracy. Does this leader of a fundamentalist school believe that the NASB or any other English translation is more accurate? If this writer believed that the text of Westcott-Hort and the NASB Bible was more accurate than the KJV, he would use them without exception.

Consistency, thou art a jewel.

There are thousands of reasons against the practice of using two different texts.

Dr. D.A. Waite says that the Westcott-Hort Text changes the Textus Receptus in 5,604 places:

- 1,952 omissions
- 467 additions
- 3,185 changes (*Defending the King James Bible*, p. 41)

Translation methods

Besides using the corrupt Westcott-Hort Revised Text, the NIV uses a technique called *Dynamic Equivalency* when translating Scriptures (dynamic = moving or changing). Dynamic Equivalency is a method of naturalistic Bible translation that adapts Scriptures to the cultural and educational level of the people. It is the same thing as paraphrasing that is used in most of the Modern English Bibles such as Kenneth Taylor's *Living Bible*. In the dynamic equivalency technique, the translators read the passage and interpret it according to their understanding. In other words, it is "idea" or "thought" translation. Of course, NIV's dynamic equivalency method is not translation; it is closer to interpretation. Actually, the editors of the NIV plainly admit that their mode of translation was geared to the "thoughts" of the writers (p. Viii of the preface of the *1969 NIV* and P. x of the *NIV Women's Devotional Bible)*. NIV has over 6,653 examples of dynamic equivalency. Simplicity is a great thing, but it is not the primary goal of a Bible translation. You may be able to understand the idea or thought of the modernistic interpretation, but it just may be the wrong thought.

If your contemporary English translation reads just like the daily newspaper, you most likely do not have an accurate Bible (God did not give the originals in modern English). Although parts of the Bible (as John's Gospel) are written in simple language and easy to understand, other parts are complex and require much study and prayer (2 Timothy 2:15; I Corinthians 2:10-16). A casual surface reading is insufficient for knowing and understanding the basic important (cardinal) truths of Scriptures.

Note: The method of Dynamic equivalency can also be found in the KJV, but it is at a very minimum. Instead of translating the "word[s]," a short "expression" is translated.

Examples:

- The expression "May the king live," is translated in the KJV as "God save the king" (I Samuel 10:24; 2 Samuel 16:16; 2 Kings 11:12; 2 Chronicles 23:11). Similar translations are also found in I Kings 1:25, 34, 39 pertaining to King Adonijah and King Solomon.
- "Hallelujah" is translated "Praise ye the Lord" (Psalms 112:1; 113:1, 9; 115:18; 116:19; 117:2; 135:1, 21...).
- "Oh that" is translated as "would God" (Numbers 11:29).

Formal Equivalency or Verbal Technique

The King James Bible uses Formal Equivalency or Verbal Technique in its translation. (Verbal technique equals same or unchanging.)

The goal of Bible translation is faithfulness to the eternal **Words of God**. The verbal equivalency technique is based upon the best English word or expression equivalency of the Greek and Hebrew words according to the context, not thoughts and ideas. Thoughts and ideas are formed by the very words that produce them; consequently, ideas, teachings, and thoughts are only true if the inspired and preserved words are accurately translated. Of course, formal equivalency technique is translation, not interpretation.

The translators of the NIV are careful not to change some of the very familiar verses such as Genesis 1:1 and John 1:1. Most people could easily detect a meaningful change in these familiar verses. Although the NIV accurately translates many verses, many other verses are mis-translations of such a subtle nature that a casual reader will not detect them. In other words, the NIV "**contains** the Word of God" but "it is **not** the whole Word of God." This is the equivalent thing that our Westcott-Hort brethren are saying about the King James Bible. Obviously, it now appears that some of our fundamentalists are beginning to say the same thing as the liberals concerning the King James.

"Now the serpent was more subtil..." - Genesis 3:1.

The Canon of Scripture

Do we have a preserved Bible text in a single canon (authoritative list of books accepted as Holy Scriptures)?

Some fundamentalist brethren believe that the inspired original Scriptures are contained somewhere within 500-5,000 manuscripts (*The Truth About The King James Version Controversy*, p. 13). According to this idea, it is up to the professors (or us) to determine the whereabouts of the originals among the numerous texts. Of course, this would be an impossible task for all of the Hebrew and Greek scholars of all ages combined together in a single generation. This Westcott-Hort fundamentalist brother believes that only the teaching is preserved (*The Truth about King Version Controversy*, pp. 12, 13). This is equivalent to the NIV's "thought" translation technique (p. viii of the 1969 *NIV* and p. x of the *NIV Women's Devotional Bible*).

Dr. Custer says, "...God's Word is preserved in the sum-total of all the manuscripts (over 5,000) which have been so far discovered" *(The Truth About The King James Version Controversy*, p. 13). Apparently, the leadership of this school agrees with him. The writer believes that God has preserved His Words in the canon of manuscripts from which our King James Bible was translated (ben Chayyim Masoretic Hebrew and Byzantine Greek).

The Hebrew and Greek texts of the Authorized King James Bible are the same texts that have been used by fundamentalist Christians down through the centuries.

Dr. Custer goes on to quote writers, Russ and Nettles (*Baptists and the Bible*, Chicago: Moody, 1980, p. 403) who say, "The truest interpretation of a passage is that which most accurately reflects the meaning of the original word."

• Although this statement is true, it is also pure hype. Who has the originals? Of course, no one does! So how do we go about making a comparison with the originals to determine what the originals are if no one has the originals? This is another *straw man* that diverts attention from God's preserved Words as found in the Hebrew and Greek texts from which the King James Bible was translated. The crux of the whole matter between traditional fundamentalists and the new breed of fundamentalists concerns the preference of the Hebrew and Greek texts.

• Of course, God inspired His original Words, but God also preserved His Words for us today in both Hebrew and Greek texts. If this were not true, Christendom would be in absolute tumult and total confusion.

Is the writer questioning the character of the Westcott-Hort fundamentalist brethren?

The writer is not questioning the integrity of Dr. Stewart Custer, his school's president, nor any others on the staff of his school. He believes that these men have excellent character but are deceived about Bible texts. By faith in God's faithfulness to preserve His Word as He promised, the writer reserves the right to disagree with these men in the area of Bible texts and translations. The writer is also saddened to see Dr. Custer's great school promote the Westcott-Hort text in the classroom. Obviously, some men become educated beyond their control.

Alfred Martin says, "The present generation of Bible students, having been reared on Westcott and Hort, have for the most part accepted the theory without independent or critical examination. To the average student of the Greek New Testament today it is unthinkable to question the theory at least in its basic premises. Even to imply that one believes the Textus Receptus to be nearer the original text than the Westcott-Hort text is, lays one open to the suspicion of gross ignorance or unmitigated bigotry. That is why this controversy needs to be aired again among Bible-believing Christians" *(Which Bible?,* p. 151).

The writer makes no claim of being an authority on Hebrew and Greek manuscripts, but he does believe that God has led him to write this paper to alert those who would follow the leadership of the Holy Spirit rather than following the biased scholarship of beguiled men. Neither has the writer ever been prejudiced against Dr. Custer's school in any way, but quite to the contrary! The writer has openly defended Custer's school for over 30 years and has even lost a few friendships because of that stand. However, the writer's allegiance will continue to be with the Traditional Text (Textus Receptus) of the King James Bible.

We are told repeatedly throughout the Bible that it is the Word(s) of the Lord:

- **Deuteronomy** 6:6: "...these Words, which I command thee this day..."

- **Deuteronomy** 8:3: "...man doth not live by bread only, but by **every Word** that
    proceedeth out of the mouth of the LORD..." (Jesus quotes this verse in Matthew
4:4; Luke 4:4.)

- **Psalms** 12:6: "the Words of the LORD are pure Words..."

- **Isaiah** 40:8: "...the Word of our God shall stand for ever."

- **Ezekiel** 12:17: "...the Word of the LORD came to me, saying..."

- **John** 6:63 - "...the Words that I (Jesus) speak unto you, they are spirit, and they
    are life."

- **I Peter** 1:25: "...the Word of the Lord endureth forever...."

- **I Peter** 1:23: "Being born again...by the Word of God..."

Other references to the Word(s) of the Lord:

Exodus 4:28; 19:6-7; 20:1; 24:3; 24:4; 34:1; **Numbers** 11:24; **Deuteronomy** 11:18; 18:18; 27:8; 28:14, 58; 29:29; **Joshua** 3:9; **I Samuel** 15:1; **II King** 22:13; **II Chronicles** 34:21; **Ezra** 7:11; 9:4; **Nehemiah** 8:13; **Job** 6:10; 19:23; 23:12; **Psalms** 119:130; **Isaiah** 51:16; **Jeremiah** 1:9; 7:27; 11:3, 6; 13:10; 16:10; 19:2; 23:30, 36; 26:2; 36:28; **Ezekiel** 2:7; 3:4; 33:32; **Amos** 8:11; **Zechariah** 7:7; **Matthew** 24:35; **Mark** 8:38; 13:31; **Luke** 9:26; 21:33; 24:8; **John** 3:34; 8:47; 12:48; 14:10, 23; 15:7; 17:8; **Acts** 15:15;

I Corinthians 2:13; **I Thessalonians** 4:18; **I Timothy** 4:6; 6:3; **II Timothy** 1:13; **2 Peter** 3:2; **Jude** 1:17; **Revelation** 1:3; 22:18-19.

There are many other references to the Word(s) of the Lord.

- The messages of God were always of exact and pure Words (Psalms 12:6).
- Pure Words make pure messages (Psalms 119:105, 169).
- The entrance of God's Words gives light and understanding to the simple (Psalms 119:130).

- **Jesus** is called The Word (Logos) in John 1:1, 14 (not an idea, thought, or concept).
- **Jesus** is called The Word of God in Revelation 19:13.

Jesus is not the "thought" of God, Jesus is the Word of God. The words (verbal) and the completed text (plenary) of the Hebrew and Greek texts underlying the King James Bible have been preserved by God and are true and faithful. Jesus said that every Word was breathed out of the mouth of God - (Matthew 4:4; Luke 4:4).

-See also Deuteronomy 8:3; 18:18.

God honors His Word above His own Name:

- **Psalms 138:2b:** For Thou hast magnified Thy Word above all Thy Name.

- If God honors His Word so greatly, why would He allow it to be hidden among 5,000 manuscripts?

(**Note:** For a more thorough study on Bible texts, refer to David W. Cloud's, *Way of Life*

Encyclopedia of the Bible and Christianity, pp. 111-126. The writer is also greatly

indebted to Dr. Donald A. Waite, David Otis Fuller, Dr. James H. Sightler, Dr. William

P. Grady, and significant others for much of the material included in this writing. All are

included in the bibliography.)

- The NIV paraphrases over 6,653 times (*Four Reasons For Defending The*

King James Bible, p. 21)

- The NIV has 4,607 translation errors (*NIV Inclusive Language Edition*, p.5)

- The NIV has 64,098 missing words (*New Age Bible Versions*, p. 28)

The NIV flagrantly omits seventeen entire verses in the New Testament and the silence in Christendom is deafening. Where are the outcries and protests that we should be hearing from our "so-called" spiritual leaders?

See if you can find these missing verses in your NIV:
- Matthew 17:21; Matthew 18:11; Matthew 23:14
- Mark 7:16; Mark 9:44, 46; Mark 11:26; Mark 15:28
- Luke 17:36; Luke 23:17
- John 5:4
- Acts 8:37; Acts 15:34; Acts 24:7; Acts 28:29
- Romans 16:24
- I John 5:7

As one writer says, "There are only four possible answers to these missing verses":

1.) The King James Greek text is correct, and the NIV Greek text is incorrect.

2.) The NIV Greek text is correct, and the King James Greek text is incorrect.

3.) Both texts of the King James and the NIV are wrong. (But this cannot be true because God promised to preserve His Word. Psalms 12:6-7; Isaiah 40:8; Matthew 24:35; I Peter 1:25.)

4.) Both texts of the King James and the NIV are correct. (But both of the texts cannot be correct since they disagree with each other thousands of times.)

The writer does not hesitate in advocating the King James Greek Text, answer No. 1.

You are obligated to search out the matter, for you must give an account to God.

- Romans 14:12: So then every one of us shall give account of himself to God.
- Romans 14:10: "...For we shall all stand before the judgment seat of Christ."

The absence of these verses in the NIV should be enough evidence to trouble the heart of even a carnal Christian.

Besides the missing verses, NIV separates Mark 16:9-20 stating, "The earliest manuscripts and some other ancient witnesses do not have Mark 16:9-20."
- This destroys the authority of the passage in the mind of the unsuspecting reader.

NIV also does the same with other passages such as Matthew 12:47; Matthew 21:44; Luke 22:43-44; John 7:53-8:11.

The writer concedes that the corrupt codices, Vaticanus and Siniaticus, may not include these verses. After all, these are the two principal sources of the Westcott-Hort Greek text that underlie the NIV.

NIV and the "Only Begotten Son"

NIV cleverly waters down the Only Begotten Son (John 1:14, 18; 3:16, 18) with, "one and only." This creates error. Christ is not the only Son of God.

Angels and men are referred to as sons of God:

• Angels are called sons of God (Job 1:6; 2:1; 38:7). Angels were created beings. Since false religions teach that Jesus was a created being, (Arianism), they feel comfortable in their theology.

(**Arianism** is the teaching of Arius, who was a priest of Alexandria, Egypt around AD 318. He and his followers denied the deity of Jesus. Arius taught that Jesus was not eternal, was created by God the Father, and was inferior to Him. *World Book Encyclopedia,* © Copyright 1980, Vol. 1, p. 625.)

• There are the sons of God who took the daughters of men for wives (Genesis 6:2).

• NT Christians are called sons of God (Philippians 2:15; John 1:12; I John 3:1- 2).

• Even Adam is called the Son of God (Luke 3:38).

• John 1:18 clarifies the only begotten.

• Hebrews 1:5: For unto which of the angels said he at any time, Thou art my Son, this day have I begotten thee? And again, I will be to him a Father, and he shall be to me a Son?

Hebrews 1:5 is a quotation from Psalms 2:7 that points to the day of Jesus' resurrection when He was begotten again from the dead. Refer to Acts 13:33 and Colossians 1:18.

• Jesus has, neither beginning of days, nor end of life (Hebrews 7:3).

• But thou, Bethlehem Ephratah, though thou be little among the thousands of Judah, yet out of thee shall he (Jesus) come forth unto me that is to be ruler in Israel;

whose goings forth have been from of old, from everlasting (Micah 5:2).

As John 1:18 declares, *"...the only begotten Son, which is in the bosom of the Father..."*

Christ is not the only Son of God, but He is The Only Begotten Son of God just as it is in the Textus Receptus and the KJV. Only Begotten Son includes the deity of Jesus in His resurrection power.

False leaders

Kurt Koch says that it is one of Satan's specialties to hide under a *Christian disguise.*

- **Jesus said,**

> ***"Beware of false prophets, which come to you in sheep's clothing, but inwardly they are ravening wolves. Ye shall know them by their fruits..." - Matthew 7:15-16.***

The writer is certain that Satan, that old serpent, has conjured up his scribes to corrupt the Word of God. The evil scribes came with swords to seize the Living Word (John 1:1) in the Garden of Gethsemane (Matthew 26:36, 47). Now, the latter day pseudo-scribes are using the printing press to attack the Written Word. The pen of the modern-day scribe may be mightier than the sword in carnal philosophies, but it is no match for the Word of God (Hebrews 4:12) that shall not pass away (Matthew 24:35).

Jude 4: "For there are certain men crept in unawares...."

Arrogant scribes believe that the Scriptures are subject to them. Wonder why NIV deletes, *"Woe unto you scribes...hypocrites...yea shall receive the greater damnation"--Matthew 23:14.*

In the Gospels, it is evident that the scribes were of the chief enemies of Christ. See Matthew 5:20; 7:29; 9:3; 12:38; 16:21; 20:18; 23:13-15, 23-29; 26:3-4; Mark 8:31; 11:18; 14:1; Luke 20:19, 46; 23:10.

The *thee* and *ye* of the King James Bible

Many people object to the *thee* and *ye* of the King James Bible but fail to realize that the King James Bible uses *you* about 2,000 times. The pronoun *ye* denotes second person plural while the pronoun *thee* denotes second person singular.

(**Note:** *You* and *your* may indicate either second person singular or second person plural in modern English.)

Singular and plural can be important in certain places such as in Matthew 16 where *ye, you, thee,* and *thou,* are used about 27 times in 23 verses.

In the King James Bible:

- Pronouns beginning with the letter *t (thee, thy, thyself, thou, thine)* denote second person singular and always refer to one person.
- Pronouns beginning with the letter *y (ye, you, your, yours, yourselves)* denote second person plural and always refer to more than one person.
- In this way, pronouns that are singular or plural are easily identified.

In John 3:7, the King James has a singular pronoun *thee* and a plural pronoun *ye*. The NIV has two *yous* instead. The singular and the plural could be confused here. So, at times, you would not know the number of persons being addressed without the *ye* and *thee*. The King James is more precise.

Besides, *thee* and *ye* are not just words of Elizabethan or Shakespearean English. Elizabethan English is Bible English. Reliable Bible scholars say that *ye* and *thee* are true translations of the Hebrew and Greek language.

(Elizabethan period: generally recognized as 1558-1642. Queen Elizabeth died in 1603.)

Readability of the King James Bible versus the NIV

What are the motives for people buying the NIV? Although the writer was quite sure of the reason, he asked people why they bought a NIV Bible. Without exception, the answer was, "It is easier to read." At times, this may appear to be true if the reader is not concerned about accuracy! However, this is not true even if accuracy is not the issue! The King James Bible has a better readability than the NIV. The King James uses one or two syllable words while the NIV uses multi-syllable words. In the *Flesch-Kincaid* research company's Grade Level Indicator, the KJV ranks easier in 23 out of 26 comparisons (*New Age Bible Versions*, pp. 195-217).

The King James also has a better readability index than the NIV in the *Right Writer* computer program. Computer programs are 100% impartial.

Following are some word comparisons of the KJV and the NIV

REFERENCE	NIV	KJV
II Chronicles 2:2	Conscripted	told
Ephesians 4:16	supporting ligament joint	fitly joined together
Luke 10:35	reimburse	repay
Luke 11:26	final condition	last state
Hebrews 1:3	representation	image
Hebrews 1:3	provided purification	purged
Hebrews 5:10	designated	Called
Hebrews 8:13	obsolete	old

Many like to find fault with the King James Bible because some of the words are considered archaic. This is not the fault of the King James Bible because it did not 'move;' the English language 'moved' (changed)! Even beginner Bible students know that some of the English words in the King James Bible have changed their meaning since 1611. A sincere Bible student will fare much better by studying out the meaning of the outdated words as opposed to trusting the critical text interpretations as found in the NIV which are derived from the corrupt Westcott-Hort/Nestle-Aland Text.

• If a person is not willing to give time to diligent study (led of the Spirit of God); he will not understand the Bible no matter which translation (or interpretation) he uses.

(Note: A list of definitions from the King James Bible, "4,114 Definitions from the Defined King James Bible," can be ordered from The Old Paths Publications website here: Dr. D.A. Waite Books (theoldpathspublications.com)"

- Also, *The Defined King James Bible* can be ordered from the Dean Burgon Society or The Old Paths Publications. The Defined King James Bible has the meaning of the outdated word on the same page that the word occurs.
- The writer also recommends the *American Dictionary of the English Language – Noah Webster 1828*. This dictionary was produced during the years when the American home, Churches, and school was established upon a Biblical and a patriotic basis.)

NIV's prominence in Christendom

While visiting Churches in his hometown and surrounding areas, this writer was made aware of the prominence given to the NIV by many different denominations. Many of the songbooks (most printed by the Nashville Press) included a Scripture verse from the NIV with every song.

(**Note**: As most Church members are probably aware, songbooks can be bought that have a corresponding Bible verse reference [with each song selection] from a selected Bible version or with Bible verses with a combination of Bible version references.)

In one church, the pastor read his text from the NIV for the communion service. This was confusing for those of us using a King James Bible. (God is not the author of confusion, I Corinthians 14:33.) Since this was a communion service, the pastor read the Scripture from I Corinthians 11:24.

- The **KJV** says, *"This is my body, which is broken for you."*

- The **NIV** says, "This is my body, which is for you."

- The Interlinear Literal Translation of the Greek New Testament (Berry) says, "This of me is the body which for you {is} being broken."

The Greek word "klao" (to break, as bread) is deleted in the NIV version. The writer does not know if the NIV translators deleted "is broken" or if they accurately translated from the corrupt 1881 Westcott-Hort revised text. Christ's body (flesh, not His bones) had to be broken. His sufferings were prophesied in Old Testament Scriptures (Isaiah 53; Psalms 22). Jesus Himself prophesied the same in the Gospels of the New Testament. God's wrath against sin could only be satisfied by an absolutely perfect sacrifice, His Only Begotten Son.

God's Son was compelled to bear the sins for many because:

- No one else was worthy.

- The prophecies (Scriptures) regarding His sufferings could not be broken (John 10:35).

This writer dearly regards the broken body (precious sufferings) of the Lord Jesus Christ. It is not redundant to repeatedly proclaim, *"Christ died for our sins"* (1 Corinthians 15:3). Apparently, the NIV translators do not regard Christ's sufferings, as does this writer, or else they are using the wrong Greek text.

Since that occasion, the writer has visited many of the Churches in and around the Greenville, SC area and noted that the majority use a New Age Bible. The NIV was the favorite corrupted bible by most.

• The writer has found very few independent Baptist Churches that use or endorse a New Age Bible version. The writer has observed that the only independent Baptist Churches that use a New Age Bible were Churches with a congregation consisting largely of college students, college graduates, and university professors.

• This writer has found many Southern Baptist and Pentecostal Churches (Assembly of God, Church of God, etc.) that use the King James translation. However, many of these churches also use the NIV, NKJV, or some other New Age Bible.

• The writer has not found a charismatic church that uses the King James Bible. However, perhaps some do.

"... *For that day shall not come, except there come a falling away first (2 Thessalonians 2:3).*

On one occasion (in a Bible bookstore), this writer was reminded of NIV's popular acceptance in Christendom when the writer's wife was attempting to select a greeting card for a friend. She observed that every card that she looked at featured a NIV Bible verse. The writer checked the very large assortment of cards -- anniversary, birthday, wedding, sympathy, graduation, etc.-- and noted the same; all the cards in every selection used a verse from the NIV. The writer has also observed that several other card companies use NIV verses. It is getting difficult to find Christmas cards with King James verses; however, many have NIV or NKJ verses.

Is it wise to buy a New Age Bible before investigating?

Warren Weirs warns in his *Confident Living* magazine: "Today there are many Bible translations, versions and paraphrases coming off the press. I am appalled to see how fickle and foolish some Christians are to run out and buy the latest version or paraphrase of the Bible thinking it is some shortcut to a spiritual experience. That isn't so, my friend. The conversion of every sinner is the call to God to holiness" (*New Age Bible Versions*, pp. 162-163).

Actually, many well-meaning Christians have purchased the NIV, believing it to be an accurate contemporary English Bible that was easier to understand. They were not trying to take a shortcut to spirituality; they just wanted a Bible in Modern English. Most were motivated to buy a NIV through the influence of either uninformed or indifferent religious leaders. These new NIV owners were either too busy to investigate or lacked concern. This writer might feel a note of sadness knowing that a pastor had studied the origin of the NIV and then made a bad choice in selecting it. However, the writer has not been told by any pastor or any other user of the NIV that they had even investigated it before using it.

Substitutions, changes, and false assumptions of the NIV

- **Micah 5:2:** NIV changes "everlasting" to "ancient times."

   In this prophecy of Christ, doubt is cast upon His eternal pre-existence. The unsuspecting reader would not realize this. Jesus shared glory with God the Father before the world was (John 17:5).

- **Mark 1:2-3:** The KJV says that Mark is quoting the "prophets," but NIV says he is quoting Isaiah the prophet.

   But Mark is not quoting just Isaiah, he is also quoting Malachi 3:1. Consequently, Mark was quoting "the prophets" just as the KJV said.

- **Ephesians 5:9:** NIV substitutes "fruit of the light" for "fruit of the Spirit."

   This fits well with mystical lights reported to have been seen at apparitions of the "Virgin." Also, it has been reported that mystical lights have been seen at cult meetings and occult initiations. Satan is the great imitator as well as the great deceiver and father of lies.

- **I Corinthians 7:1:** NIV changes "touch" to "marry."

   The Greek word for touch, "haptomai," is in the Traditional Greek Text for this passage:

   The Greek word for marry, "gameo," is not.

While Paul would have desired for the "then present distress" that all men were unmarried as himself, he was not teaching this for all time (I Corinthians 7: 7-9, 26-29).

Paul even warns against forbidding to marry

I Timothy 4:1-3: "Now the Spirit speaketh expressly, that in the latter times some shall depart from the faith, giving heed to seducing spirits, and doctrines of devils; Speaking lies in hypocrisy; having their conscience seared with a hot iron; Forbidding to marry and..."

Hebrews 13:4: Marriage is honourable in all, and the bed undefiled: but whoremongers and adulterers God will judge.

Neither does Paul advocate celibacy for pastors (bishops)

"A bishop must be the husband of one wife and having his children in subjection"
(I Timothy 3:2, 4; Titus 1:6).

Jesus Christ will forever be in flesh

• **I John 4:2-3**: NIV (also NASV and NKJV) erroneously translates Jesus Christ "has come" in the flesh, while KJV uses "is come" in the flesh.

The present-tense verb "is" carries the meaning of continuance. The past-tense verb "was" strongly suggests a discontinuance. The Word not only has been made flesh (John 1:1, 14) but is still flesh and will forever be in flesh (flesh and bone - Luke 24:39).

One reliable Bible scholar says that the perfect participle "is come" of I John 4:2 and the present participle "is come" of II John 7, have the basic meaning of "continuance" and "eternal present" and are nearly the same. Jesus did not incarnate a body for a short time only to shed it later.

Elhanan killed Goliath.

- **II Samuel 21:19:** NIV says that Elhanan killed Goliath.

A young child knows that David slew Goliath. The King James got it right. Elhanan killed Lahmi, the brother (or son) of Goliath. Refer to I Samuel 17:31-50; II Samuel 21:19, 22; I Chronicles 20:5, 8.

The KJV translates more accurately than the NIV interpretation

- **Psalms 12:7:** NIV mistranslates "us" for "them" in reference of the Words of the Lord.
- **Isaiah 14:12:** NIV confuses Jesus with Lucifer in Isaiah 14 by calling Lucifer, "O morning star."

Although Lucifer (Latin for "lightbearer") is called "son of the morning" and celestial beings are referred to as "morning stars" (Job 38:7), **Jesus is "the Morning Star" and "the Day Star"** in the Bible (Revelation 2:28; Revelation 22:16; II Peter 1:19).

- The Hebrew word for "morning" is *boqer*.
- The Hebrew word for "star" is *kokav*, or *kowkab* (plural = *kokavim*).
- There is no Hebrew word for "star" in this verse at all.

• The Hebrew word for Lucifer in Isaiah 14:12 is *helel* (or *heylel*).

Strong's Concordance translates the word *helel/heylel* as both "Lucifer" and "the morning star." Morning star is incorrect. (Lexicons and Concordances are often incorrect.)

Helel is a masculine, singular noun which is translated Lucifer in the King James Bible and means "light bearer" or "shining one" (*Analytical Hebrew and Chaldee Lexicon* by D. Davidson, published by Samuel Baxter and Sons).

"Thou hast corrupted thy wisdom by reason of thy (Lucifer's) brightness..." (Ezekiel 28:17).

D.A. Waite says that *helel* (a noun) is from the Hebrew verb *halal* which means, "to shine." It is true that stars shine, but the verb does not mean, "star" or "morning star," it only means, "to shine." So the noun version (*helel*) of the verb *halal,* means a person that shines or "shining one" (*Foes of the King James Bible Refuted*, pp. 55-57).

We are told in the New Testament that Satan himself is transformed as an angel of light (2 Corinthians 11:13-15). Satan's ministers *also* shine forth as ministers of righteousness.

A sodomite English advisor (or translator) of the NIV

One of the NIV English language advisors on the NIV translation, Dr. Virginia Mollenkott, admits her homosexuality on page 12 of her book, *Sensuous*

Spirituality {what an oxymoron!}- *New Age Bible Versions*, p. 77. The writer does not know whether or not her overt lesbianism influenced the NIV translators to render sodomite(s) as "shrine prostitute" and "male shrine prostitutes" in the following references: Deuteronomy 23:17; I Kings 14:24; 15:12; 22:46; II Kings 23:7.

Some may object to the Kings James' translation of the word *qadesh* as "sodomite" in these passages. Perhaps the main reason for questioning lies in the definitions and the way that they are given by concordances and lexicons. (Again, concordances and lexicons are not inspired.) For example, in order of mention, *Strong's Exhaustive Concordance Of The Bible* defines the word *qadesh* as a male prostitute before giving the term *sodomite.*

(*qadesh*-- Strong's Concordance # 6945: a {quasi} sacred person, i.e., {techn.} a {male} devotee {by prostitution} to licentious idolatry: --sodomite, unclean.)

This first mentioning can have the effect of shading the meaning to be somewhat different from its primary definition. In this instance, the order of mention in the lexicon may tend to make the meaning appear as though the male shrine prostitute commits natural sex sin with the opposite sex. However, the unnatural perverted same-sex relationship is meant.

The King James Bible translates all five of the aforementioned verses as sodomite(s).

Following are renderings of Qadesh in four different English Bibles

In the table, Green's refers to Green's Interlinear.

REFERENCE	KJB	GREEN'S	NIV	NASB
Deuteronomy 23:17	sodomite	homosexual	Shrine prostitute	cult prostitute
I Kings 14:24	sodomite	sodomite	male shrine prostitutes	male cult prostitutes
I Kings 15:12	sodomites	sodomites	male shrine prostitutes	male cult prostitute
I Kings 22:46	sodomites	sodomites	male shrine prostitutes	prostitutes

Looking at each of the five references in the King James Bible

• **2 Kings 23:7:** The fact that sodomites were functioning as male shrine prostitutes does not disallow the fact that they were still sodomites (homosexuals). This passage shows how bold the sodomites had become with their abominable practice in Judah. Here, they had even brought the heathen custom into the religious worship of the Jews. Of course, sodomites were scattered about in all of the land (I Kings 14:22-24; 15:12; 22:46).

• **Deuteronomy 23:17-18:** Beginning at Deuteronomy 23:14, we have the term "thy camp" twice. No mention of the house of the LORD until verses 17 and 18 where the "the price of a dog" is expressly forbidden to be put into the Temple treasury.

(Price of a dog is a figurative expression of the pay or gains of the sodomite obtained by his lewd, unclean, and dog-like practice.)

(**Note:** The "hire of a whore" and the "price of a dog" (money or gains of these immoral practices) were forbidden as an offering in the house of the Lord for any kind of vow. Both were an abomination to the LORD. Dogs compassed Jesus on the Cross of Calvary (Psalms 22:16.)

- **I Kings 14:24:** And there were also sodomites *"in the land"* and they did according to all the abominations of the nations which the LORD cast out before the children of Israel.

Notice here, that it is sodomites "in the land," not "in the Temple."

"Judah did evil in the sight of the LORD according to all the abominations of the nations which the LORD cast out before the children of Israel" (I Kings 14:22, 24).

The sodomites were "in the land," not just in or adjacent to the Temple. The book of Leviticus lists the abominable practice of the sodomites. God warned the Jews about this unnatural sin.

> *Leviticus 18:22: Thou shalt not lie with mankind as with woman kind: it is abomination.*

> *Leviticus 20:13: If a man also lie with mankind as he lieth with a woman, both of them have committed an abomination: they*

shall surely be put to death; their blood shall be upon them.

Even the NIV got these two verses correct!

I Kings 15:12: And he (Asa) took away the sodomites out of the land..."

Obviously, the sodomites were not relegated to the Temple site alone.

• **I Kings 22:46:** And the remnant of the sodomites, which remained in the days of his father Asa, he (Jehoshaphat) took out of the land.

Most likely, the first place that the godly king, Asa, would have removed the sodomites would have been in the Temple. Here, Asa's son, Jehoshaphat, removes the remnant out of the land.

The word, sodomite, is given to those who practice sodomy, the unnatural sex for which Sodom became noted.

Genesis 19:5 And they called unto Lot, and said unto him, Where are the men which came in to thee this night? bring them out unto us, that we may know them.

Sodomy was the acts and rites of unnatural sex by male temple prostitutes of heathen worship. The Jews picked up the abominable practice from the pagans. This practice is referred to in Romans 1:27.

Romans 1:27 And likewise also the men, leaving the natural use of the woman, burned in their lust one toward another; men with men working that which is

> ***unseemly, and receiving in themselves that recompence of their error which was meet.***

The writer concludes that *sodomite* is the best translation for the word *qadash* since sodomites are only associated with the temple in one verse (II Kings 23:7) and "in the land" in all of the other passages. Since the lewd acts were widespread in the land and not confined to the temple alone, it cannot be said that all the sodomites "of the land" were temple shrine prostitutes. A person indulging in the debased behavior was a sodomite whether in the temple or in the land.

The NIV does use the word *homosexual* in I Corinthians 6:9 (the word *homosexual* is of recent invention). Regarding I Corinthians 6:9, Dr. Virginia Mollenkott says the Bible only censures "homosexual offenders," not "sincere homosexuals."

It is not clear what Dr. Mollenkott meant here.

- Is she saying that the Bible only censures people who offend sincere sodomites (homosexuals)?
- On the other hand, does she mean that God censures the offending sodomite but does not censure the sincere sodomite?

If Dr. Mollenkott means that God does not censure the sincere sodomite, the writer's questions are:

- If sincere hetersexuals, who are wrong, are judged by God, why are sincere homosexuals, who are wrong, not censured?

- On the other hand, if she is saying that that the Bible only censures those who offend homosexuals, she will not be able to prove that from the Bible.

Furthermore, if it is sin, being a sincere homosexual (sodomite) or sincere heterosexual does not merit any pardon from the judgment of God. Sincerity must be based upon the Word of God. It is "godly sorrow" that worketh repentance (change of mind about sin, salvation, and judgment to come). The "sorrow of the world" worketh death (2 Corinthians 7:10).

Confession of sin and accepting Jesus' sacrifice on the cross of Calvary will save, "whosoever" (Romans 10:13).

God condemns the price of a sodomite.

In the OT, God condemns the price of a sodomite (offering) by referring to him as a dog. The price of a whore is also called an abomination.

> *Deuteronomy 23:17-18: There shall be no whore of the daughters of Israel, nor a sodomite of the sons of Israel. Thou shalt not bring the hire of a whore, or the price of a dog, into the house of the LORD thy God for any vow: for even both these are abomination unto the LORD thy God.*

Sodomy (homosexuality) is condemned as an abomination in the Book of Leviticus.

> *Leviticus 18:22: "Thou shalt not lie with mankind, as with womankind: it is abomination."*

NIV's collaborator, Dr. Virginia Mollenkott, tells of her spirit guide and communication with her dead mother in her book, *Is The Homosexual My Neighbor? (Which Bible Is God's Word*, pp. 67-68). The Bible speaks against a "necromancer" (Deuteronomy 18:11). Webster's dictionary defines necromancy as magic or sorcery; the calling up of the spirits of the dead. That is how the Bible defines it. (Westcott and Hort also dabbled in the occult through their "Ghostly Guild Club.")

A Westcott-Hort fundamentalist editor speaks

A fundamentalist Christian editor, who commends the NIV for using the word homosexual in I Corinthians 6:9, faults the King James Bible for not using the word homosexual at all. As far as the writer has been able to determine, the word *homosexual* was not invented until the 1800's (some sources say 1900's), which was about 200 years after the King James Bible. This same critic of the King James Text felt that s*odomite* did not paint a clear picture of a pervert. He says that *sodomite* may have a strong reference to the person's nationality rather than implying an immoral practice of sodomy. The writer has never met anyone who perceived a sodomite as just a resident of Sodom. The abominable practice of sodomy is obviously inferred. *Sodomite* and *sodomy* are synonymous terms that fit the perverts of nature with their perverted actions. Perhaps this Westcott-Hort fundamentalist editor would like to enlighten Webster's Dictionary. Webster defines a sodomite as one who practices sodomy, not a resident of Sodom (*Webster's Ninth New Collegiate Dictionary*, p.1120).

CHAPTER 2

NIV OMISSIONS, DELETIONS, AND SUBSTITUTIONS

- Matthew 1:25: NIV omits "firstborn" that allows for the false doctrine of perpetual virginity for Mary the mother of Jesus, which the Roman church claims for her.

The blessed Mary was not a perpetual virgin as Roman Catholicism claims. Mary had other children. Jesus had brothers and sisters (Mark 6:3).

> *"Is not this the carpenter's son? is not his mother called Mary? and his brethren, James, and Joses, and Simon, and Judas? And his sisters, are they not all with us? And they were offended at him.*
>
> *...Whence then hath this man all these things?" (Matthew 13:55-56).*
>
> *"Then one said unto him, Behold, thy mother and thy brethren stand without, desiring to speak with thee" (Matthew 12:47.*

Although Mary was well-favored of God, she was no more divine than any other great men and women of the Bible; to name a few: Job, Abraham, Isaac, Israel, Joseph, Moses, Deborah, David, Hannah, Daniel, Isaiah, Jeremiah, Esther, Noah, John the Baptist, Peter, Paul, Lydia, Dorcas, James, John, etc.

Jesus is the only person or God/man who is divine.

- **Matthew 27:4:** *"the innocent blood"* is changed to "innocent blood" in the NIV.

Many innocent men have had their blood shed. The blood of innocent animals was shed in OT atonements. Jesus is the only one with the innocent blood ("...cleanses from all sin" I John 1:7; Colossians 1:14).

- **Mark 6:11** - NIV omits, "Verily, I say unto you, It shall be more tolerable for Sodom and Gomorrha in the day of Judgment, than for that city."

- **Philippians 4:13** - "I can do all things through Christ which strengtheneth me."

NIV substitutes "him" for Christ. Him is substituted many times for Christ. This accommodates the many "hims" of international religions such as Buddhism, Islam, Hindi, etc. Satan is very subtle in his attack on Scriptures.

- **Revelation 2:15:** NIV removed the phrase, "which things I hate."

Nicolaitans is derived from two Greek words:

1.) Nico = to conquer

2.) Laity = the people (as distinguished from the clergy).

This hierarchy describes the Roman church role through the centuries. The Lord hates it. The Catholic Church has many Protestant sisters who follow her dogmas.

More NIV deletion, omission, changes, and substitutions

- **Matthew 6:13** (Lord's prayer): "For thine is the kingdom, and the power, and the

  glory, forever. Amen"-- omitted in NIV.

- **Matthew 27:34:** NIV replaces the word *vinegar* with the word *wine*.

  This creates a contradiction with the prophecy in Psalms 69:21, which says Christ was given vinegar to drink. Even NIV translates vinegar in Psalms 69:21.

- **Mark 10:21:** NIV deletes, "take up thy cross."

- **Mark 10:24:** NIV deletes, "for them that trust in riches."

- **Luke 2:33:** NIV designates Joseph as Jesus' father.

  Joseph was His foster father. Jesus was conceived of the Holy Ghost (Matthew 1:20; Luke 1:27, 35).

  One brother of the NIV persuasion commented concerning Luke 2:33, "Does the KJV open the same door in John 1:45: 6:42?" The answer is "No." John 1:45 merely reports what Philip said to Nathanael. Of course, Philip may not have understood the prophecy of Moses (and Isaiah) concerning the virgin birth of Jesus at this time. Although John 1:45 is an accurate statement of what Philip said, it is not an inspired statement of fact as is the declaration by the Holy Spirit in Luke 2:33. The serpent's lies to Eve in the Garden of Eden were not inspired of God though they were factual words of Satan. Even in the Bible, believers said and did the wrong things many times when they were not led of the Holy Spirit.

Neither does the KJV declare Jesus to be the son of Joseph in John 6:42. The ones who called Jesus the son of Joseph were unbelieving Jews who followed Jesus because of the loaves that they did eat. Even if these Jews had been believers, it would be understood that Joseph was a parent in the sense of being a foster-father of Jesus (Luke 2:27).

• **Luke 2:43:** NIV replaces "Joseph and his mother" with, "his parents."

This creates the same problem as that of Luke 2:33. This clever substitution creates an error and gives support to the modernists who deny the virgin birth (Isaiah 7:14; Galatians 4:4; Matthew 1:23; Luke 1:27).

(**Note**: Although you could prove the deity of Christ by using the NIV, you could also be misled to disprove Christ's deity by the NIV.)

• **Luke 4:4:** NIV deletes "but by every word of God" which is a quote from Deuteronomy 8:3; 18:18.

(Strangely or perhaps by an oversight, they leave it in Matthew 4:4.)

• **Luke 4:8:** NIV deletes, "...Get thee behind Me, Satan..."

- **Luke 4:18:** NIV deletes, "He hath sent me to heal the broken hearted."

- **Luke 11:2** (Lord's prayer): 14 words deleted which are related to Heaven in one single verse in the NIV.

- **John 3:13:** NIV deletes, "the Son of Man which is in heaven."

- **John 3:15:** NIV omits, "should not perish."

   The writer doubts that the NIV translators believe in a punishment in Hell (NT: Gehenna).

- **John 6:47:** NIV omits, "on me." This leaves, "He that believeth...hath everlasting life."

   Whether right or wrong, all sincere worshippers believe that their religion is true. To protest perceived injustices, many sincere *religionists* have publicly torched themselves with gasoline. Others have rushed to their death in various other ways in order to appease their heathen gods. Even some Muslims today are committed to suicide bombing.

   Before and during World War II, many devout religionists committed hara-kiri (ritual suicide) believing that they had done service for their pagan emperor god. Their sincerity is not in doubt, just their god.

   History records many instances of people taking a fatal dose of the wrong medicine for their illness. Their sincerity was placed in the wrong remedy. Believing in a false way to Heaven is even more dangerous. Just believing "something" as NIV infers in John 6:47 will not give everlasting life. The writer is not ashamed to acknowledge Jesus Christ as the only Mediator, just as it is declared in the King James Bible (I Timothy 2:5).

I Timothy 5:15: For some are already turned aside after Satan.

- **John 16:14:** "He [the Spirit of truth] shall glorify me." NIV changes to "He shall bring glory to me."

- **John 16:16:** NIV deletes, "because I go to the Father."

- **Acts 8:37:** Entire verse deleted. This is where the Ethiopian eunuch says, "I believe that Jesus Christ is the Son of God."

- **Romans 1:16:** NIV omits, "of Christ" from the "gospel of Christ."

There are many false gospels. The only true Gospel that gives eternal life and saves a soul from eternal torment in Hell is the Gospel of Christ.

- **I Corinthians 5:7:** Christ our Passover is sacrificed for us. NIV deletes "for us."

- **Galatians 4:7:** NIV drops "through Christ."

- **Ephesians 3:14:** NIV deletes, "of our Lord Jesus Christ."

- **Ephesians 3:9:** "God, who created all things by Jesus Christ. NIV deletes, "by Jesus Christ." (Could it be that the NIV does not acknowledge that Jesus Christ is God?)

- **Colossians 1:14:** In whom we have redemption through His blood. NIV deletes, "through His blood."

Did the Westcott-Hort Greek text include blood here, or were the NIV "interpreters" unconcerned with Christ's precious shed blood?

- **I Timothy 3:16; Revelation 21:4:** "He" substituted for "God."

Again, he or him could be used of any false god.

- **Hebrews 1:3:** "by Himself purged our sins." NIV deletes "by Himself."

This allows room for the co-mediatrix (female mediator), Mary. The Bible teaches that there is **only ONE MEDIATOR** between God and man – **JESUS** (Acts 4:12; I Timothy 2:5; John 14:6).

- **I Peter 4:1:** Christ hath suffered for us. NIV drops, "for us."

- **II Peter 1:21:** "holy men of God spake." NIV deletes, "holy" as in many other places.

- **2 John 5:7:** Robs part of verse 8 to pretend a verse 7.

NIV deletes names and titles of Jesus about 144 times; sometimes an inferior title is substituted. Jesus is removed about 46 times.

NIV removed the only place in the Bible where Christ refers to Himself as "Jesus" (Matthew 16:20). The meaning of Jesus is "Jehovah is Salvation," or "Savior."

CHAPTER 3

APOLOGIST FOR THE NIV

- One of the apologists for the NIV is Jim White, a practicing Mormon.
- Bob Morey, another NIV apologist, calls the King James the Queen (which means queer) James (*Which Bible Is God's Word*, pp. 61, 63).

The haters of the preserved Masoretic and Byzantine text of the King James Bible have gone to great effort to malign the unconverted (?) King James I of England, who authorized the 1611 translation of the King James Bible, by promoting his "alleged" homosexuality. Of course, this was done to destroy the people's confidence in the Majority Text of the King James Bible that God preserved as He promised. Even if King James had been a sodomite, it would not have affected the translation of the King James Bible because he had no part in the translation itself. However, the sodomite (lesbian), Dr. Virginia Mollenkott, did have a part in NIV's English translation.

Dr. William P. Grady says, "However, to discover the vilest attacks against his person [King James I], we must look to the 20th-century writings of apostate Christians! With the major encyclopedia sets such as Americana (1991), Britannica (1992), Collier's (1990), World Book (1988), and even the Catholic Encyclopedia for Home and School (1960) completely silent on the matter, an article in *Moody Monthly* categorically reports that King James was an open homosexual. (In over twenty pages of copy, the editors of the *Dictionary of National Biography* do not so much as allude to the rumor one time" *(Final Authority,* p.147).

(The Following Copied April 20, 2006, David Cloud, *Fundamental Baptist Information Service,* **P.O. Box 610368, Port Huron, MI 48061, 866-295-4143, fbns@wayoflife.org)**

WAS KING JAMES A HOMOSEXUAL?

The accusation that King James I, who authorized the King James Bible, was a homosexual has often been made, but we need to be cautious about accepting it.

Since he fathered eight children, he couldn't have been much of a homosexual.

He wrote love letters to his wife and obviously enjoyed her most intimate company. He referred to her as "our dearest bedfellow" (Gustavus Paine, *The Men Behind the King James Version,* p. 4). When John Rainolds questioned the phrase in the Anglican marriage service, "with my body I thee worship," King James replied: "...if you had a good wife yourself, you would think that all the honor and worship you could do to her would be well bestowed."

In a book that the King wrote to his son Henry (entitled *Basilikon Doron,* or *A King's Gift*), he made the following statements about the importance of sexual purity:

"But the principal blessing [is] in your marrying of a godly and virtuous wife, being flesh of your flesh and bone of your bone. Marriage is the greatest earthly felicity" (p. 43).

"Keep your body clean and unpolluted while you give it to your wife whom to only it belongs for how can you justly crave to be joined with a Virgin if your body be polluted?" (p. 44).

"When you are married, keep inviolably our promise made to God in your marriage" (p. 45).

"Abstain from the filthy vice of adultery; remember only what solemn promise ye made to God at your marriage" (p. 54).

The King wrote plainly against the sin of homosexuality.

"Especially eschew [shun] to be effeminate" (*Basilikon Doron*, p. 46).

"There are some horrible crimes that ye are bound in conscience never to forgive: such as witchcraft, willful murder, incest, and sodomy" (p. 48).

The charge of homosexuality was made by the king's enemies and only after his death. Stephen Coston's book *King James the VI of Scotland and the I of England Unjustly Accused?* (St. Petersburg, FL: Konigswort, 1996) makes the case that the charge was slanderous and untrue. The charge was first made by Anthony Weldon, who had been expelled from his office by James for political reasons and had sworn that he would have his day of vengeance. Weldon not only hated James, he hated the entire Scottish race. Historian Maurice Lee, Jr., warned, "Historians can and should ignore the venomous caricature of the king's person and behavior drawn by Anthony Weldon" (*Great Britian's Solomon: James VI & I in His Three Kingdoms*, 1990, pp. 309-310). See also David Wilson, *King James VI & I* (New York: Oxford University Press, 1956) and Christopher Durston, *James I* (London: Routledge, 1993).

It is also important to understand that King James lived in an age in which intimate but non-sexual relationships between males was common. While at Cambridge, William Sancroft, the future Archbishop of Canterbury, had such a relationship with his roommate Arthur Bonnest. "They lived together, read together and slept together." When Bonnest contracted TB and had to leave the school, the two continued to correspond. Bonnest wrote: "Thou art oftener in my thoughts than ever; thou art nearer me than when I embraced them. Thou sayest thou lovest me; good, well repeat it again and again." Adam Nicholson, who records this from Sancroft's personal correspondence, observes: "The age was at ease with unbridled but apparently quite unsexual love between men" (*God's Secretaries*, p. 132).

While we do not believe that King James was a homosexual, we do not defend his character very far. He was a persecutor of Baptists and other separatists who refused to submit to the state church. In fact, the last two men burned alive in England for their faith were burned during the reign of James, and many others died in cruel prison cells for no crime other than following the Bible according to the dictates of their own conscience. It was because of the persecution poured out during James' reign that the Puritans fled England and sailed for America in 1607 and the Pilgrims followed in 1620.

The bottom line is that the character of King James I has no relevance to the King James Bible itself. Though he set the project in notion and there is evidence that he maintained an interest in keeping it moving along, he had no role in the translation. He did not even finance the project.

CHAPTER 4

THE WRITER'S VIEWPOINT

Satan is working overtime to pervert God's Word by forming his counterfeit *global bible* to supplant God's Word. He realizes that in order to control the religious masses of the world, he must have a generic bible acceptable to all religions.

One writer put it well when he said, "The NIV is clearly an Interdenominational Masterpiece." It certainly is a giant step toward the formation of a One-World Bible.

Recently, [October 1999] the United Nations was calling for the heads of all the major religions to come together. The United Religious Organization is scheduled to be launched in the year 2000. Could the reader venture a guess as to who will be elected to head this future Tribulation global religious organization? No, not the antichrist, but his false apostle, the beast out of the earth in Revelation 13:11, 12 who causes the world to worship the antichrist beast out of the sea of nations. The 'bride of antichrist' must have a common bible suitable for the constituency of the various religions represented. The apostate National Council of Churches of America is going to try to form a new ecumenical organization that would for the first time include all major branches of U.S. Christianity (*The Greenville News*, Section B, p. 1, May 24, 2000.)

A One-World Religion must have a One-World Bible. The translators, editors, publishers, and promoters of modern new age bible **per**-versions are pioneering the way for antichrist. They are twisting the pages of Holy Scriptures to facilitate the acceptance of all false gods and blind followers.

Truth and error cannot be mixed.

"Thy Word is Truth" (John 17:17).

An International Version (or, **N**ew **I**nternational **V**ersion) or Global bible will be instrumental in deceiving a major part of the whole world in the end time. Many souls will be damned during the tribulation period because they received not the love of the truth.

> ***2 Thessalonians 2:3, 9-12: Let no man deceive you by any means: for that day shall not come, except there come a falling away first, and that man of sin be revealed, the son of perdition. Even him, whose coming is after the working of Satan with all power and signs and lying wonders. And with all deceivableness of unrighteousness in them that perish; because they received not the love of the truth, that they might be saved. And for this cause God shall send them strong delusion, that they should believe a lie; That they all might be damned who believed not the truth but had pleasure in unrighteousness.***

Again, perhaps Antichrist's chief minister, the False Prophet of Revelation 13:11-15, will be elected as the head of the World Religious Organization some time beyond the year 2000. The writer has little doubt as to the identity of this false prophet.

NIV editor's comments

• Calvin Linton says that the translator's own interpretation may color the text or even misrepresent it (*New Age Bible Versions*, p. 392).

• Ronald Youngblood says, "It may be true at times that the NIV translators have been guilty of reading something into the text" (*New Age Bible Versions*, p. 394).

• The NIV's Concordance editor says, "Translations do evidence the theological convictions of their translators...It is complex because of individuals who favor one Bible over another for theological reasons and publishers who promote one version over another at least partly for economic reasons" (*Words About the Word*, pp. 54, 74).

Such new age version editors join those who, according to Lola Davis, are unconsciously preparing mankind for a World Religion that is compatible with the New Age (*New Age Bible Versions*, p. 11).

• Edwin Palmer says that [there are] few clear and decisive texts that declare that Jesus is God (*New Age Bible Versions*, p. 231).

Palmer should have said this for the New Age Bible versions.

Verses That Teach the Deity of Jesus

The writer has compiled several pages of Bible verses that teach the Deity of Jesus. One verse is sufficient. Following are a few of those verses:

Isaiah 7:14; 9:6; Psalms 22; 110:1; Zechariah 3:2; Matthew 1:16, 23; 16:16, 20; 26:65; Mark 14:61-64; Luke 22:70-71; 23:1-3; John 1:1, 3, 10, 14; 5:18, 22-23; 6:46; 8:58; 10:30; 11:25-26; 14:9; 17:5, 24; 19:7; Acts 2:36; I Corinthians 5:7; 15:47; I Timothy 3:16; 6:14-16; Philippians 2:6; Colossians 1:15; 2:9; 16:2, 9; Titus 2:13; Hebrews 1:3, 8; 13:8; I John 3:16; Revelation 4:6; 20:6.

The Creator is God

Certainly, the Creator is God. Many times, we are told that Jesus created all things:

John 1:10: *"... the world was made by Him..."*

I Corinthians 8:6: *"...one Lord Jesus Christ, by whom are all things..."*

Colossians 1:16: *"...by Him were all things created..."*

Hebrews 1:10: *"And, Thou, Lord, in the beginning hast laid the foundation of the earth..."*

Revelation 4:11: *"...for thou hast created all things..."*

Also see Revelation 10:6; 14:6-7; 21:5-7; 22:3.

Jesus is called LORD 663 times

Jesus is called LORD 663 times. Competent Bible scholars say that the Greek word *Kurios* is equivalent of the Hebrew word *Adonai* that was used by Jesus in Matthew 22:43-45. This is where Jesus is quoting David in Psalms 110:1. The Pharisees did not believe that Jesus was the Son of David, who was the Son of God, who was the Messiah.

Apparently, Palmer does not feel strongly about the deity of Christ. Then, neither does the NIV! The central theme of Scriptures is Jesus Christ and all Scriptures have their fulfillment in Him. The writer believes that Jesus is the Christ of God.

I John 5:1: *"Whosoever believeth that Jesus is the Christ is born of God..."*

I John 4:3: *"And every spirit that confesseth not that Jesus Christ is come in the flesh is not of God..."*

John 8:24: *"...for if ye believe not that I am he, ye shall die in your sins."*

CHAPTER 5

NEW AGE BIBLES & 'THE WAY'

The NIV capitalizes "Way" in Acts 9:2; 19:9, 23; 22:4; 24:14, 22. Again, this patronizes major false religions of the world as well as many cults and occults.

- Buddhism calls itself, "The Way."
- Shinto (Japan) means, "The Way of the gods." They worship a sun goddess.
- Taoism is Chinese for, "The Way."
- Hinduism is defined as "The Way" of the majority of people in India, a Way.
- Ancient Gnosticism was called, "The Way."
- Islam uses the term, the Way, a Way in their Sufi branch.
- The Way is a New Age Luciferian term.

The "ONLY Way"

JESUS CHRIST Is The "ONLY Way" to God the Father.

> *John 14:6: Jesus saith unto him, I am the way, the truth, and the life: no man cometh unto the Father, but by me.*

> *Acts 4:12: Neither is there salvation in any other: for there is none other name under heaven given among men, whereby we must be saved.*

Capitalizing 'Virgin' in reference to Mary

NIV capitalizes *virgin* in the following passages: II Kings 19:21; Isaiah 23:12; 37:22; 47:1; Jeremiah 18:13; 31:4,21; 46:11; Lamentations 1:15; 2:13; Amos 5:2, and then omits "by Himself" in Hebrews 1:3.

Can the reader guess why? The capitalization of *virgin* (for Mary) plus the deletion of the purging of our sin "by himself" (Jesus) leaves room for the Marian doctrine commonly referred to as "**Mariolatry**." This is the idolatrous worship of Mary. According to Roman Catholicism's "Immaculate Conception" doctrine, Mary was born without the original taint of sin (*The World Book Encyclopedia*, Copyright 1980, Vol. 10, and p. 67).

Note: Mary's perpetual virginity was decreed by the Council of Chalcedon in 451 A.D. (*New Age Bible Versions*, p. 109).

Mary was not a **co-mediatrix** or co-redemptress with Christ. Although Mary was greatly blessed of God, she was born a sinner as are all other people and needed a Savior, as do all other people. Even Adam and Eve, who were not born of woman (as Mary was), were sinners and needed a sin covering. Since Mary was a natural born, she was a sinner by nature. Mary (although pure) did not live an absolutely sinless life.

Jesus was conceived without sin (conceived of the Holy Ghost) and lived without sin (John 8:46; Hebrews 4:15).

If Mary needed a Savior, she must have been a sinner

Luke 1:46-48: And Mary said, My soul doth magnify the Lord. And my spirit hath rejoiced in God my Saviour. For He hath regarded the low estate of his handmaiden; for, behold, from henceforth all generations shall call me blessed.

More than 100 times, the following names and titles of Jesus are deleted by the NIV:

Jesus; Christ; God; Lord; Master; Good Master; Jesus Christ; Christ Jesus; Lord Jesus; Lord Jesus Christ; the Son; His Son; Beloved Son; the Word; Prophet; Holy Child; Son of Man; Son of God; Son of the Living God; Just Person; Bridegroom; the Beginning and the Ending; Alpha and Omega; the First and the Last, etc.

See **Matthew** 8:29; 9:28; 13:36, 51; 15:30; 16:20; 17:20, 22; 18:2, 11; 19:16; 23:8, 10; 24:2; 25:13; 27:24; 28:6; **Mark** 2:19; 5:13; 7:27; 9:24; 11:10, 14; 14:18, 45; **Luke** 4:41; 7:22, 31; 9:35, 56; 13:25; 17:6; 22:31; 23:42; **John** 4:16, 42, 46; 6:69; 8:20, 35; 9:35; 11:14, 39; 13:23; 19:38; 20:15; 21:5, 21; **Acts** 2:30; 3:13, 23, 26; 4:27, 30; 7:30; 8:37; 9:5-6, 29; 15:11, 18; 16:31; 19:4, 10; 20:21; 22:16; **Romans** 1:16; 6:11; 14:6; 15:8; 16:18, 20, 24; **I Corinthians** 5:4-5; 9:1, 18; 10:28; 15:23, 47; 16:22-23; **II Corinthians** 4:6, 10, 11; 5:18; 10:7; 11:31; **Galatians** 3:17; 4:7; 6:15, 17; **Ephesians** 3:9, 14; **Philippians** 4:13; **Colossians** 1:2, 28; **I Thessalonians** 1:1; 2:19; 3:11, 13;

II Thessalonians 1:8, 12; **I Timothy** 1:1; 2:7; 3:16; 5:21; **II Timothy** 4:1; **Philemon** 6; **Hebrews** 3:1; 10:30; **I**

Peter 3:15; 5:10, 14; **I John** 1:7; 4:3; 5:7, 13; **II John** 3, 9; **Revelation** 1:8-9, 11, 13; 12:17; 14:14; 20:12, 21

However, there are over 300 additional titles (Jesus, Christ, and Lord) in the NIV. None of these can be found in the Traditional Text and are not italicized to indicate that they were added. Many replaced pronouns that already clearly pointed to Christ.

NIV omits references to "Jesus Christ," "The Lord," or "God," 173 times (*Which Bible Is God's Word*, p. 85).

The Godhead:

Acts 17:29: NIV changes Godhead (capital G) to "divine being" (small "d" and small "b").

Romans 1:20: NIV changes Godhead (capital G) to "divine nature" (small "d" and small "n").

(2 Peter 1:4 says we are partakers of "divine nature," but hardly on the level with God.)

Colossians 2:9: NIV changes Godhead to "Deity" (capital "D").

The following chart is copied from D. A. Waite's *Defending The King James Bible*, p. 128:

Words in KJV	Times in KJV	Times in NIV
Advocate	1	0
Chaste	3	0
Concupiscence	3	0
Sodomite(s)	5	0
Carnal/carnality	15	0
Impute/imputation	15	0
Fornication	44	0
Abiding	55	0

Are the original manuscripts the only Scriptures that can be trusted?

"Only the original autographs are inerrant."

When any controversy arises concerning the authority of Scriptures, most fundamental Bible believers have been indoctrinated to rely on the catch phrase, "Only the original autographs are inerrant." A good man, Benjamin B. Warfield of Princeton University (1887-1921), introduced this statement of belief to modern fundamentalism. Dr. Warfield became concerned that the discovery of other manuscripts, especially Vaticanus and Sinaiticus, might offer more accuracy than the Masoretic and Byzantine manuscripts of the AV (KJV). To solve his *alleged* dilemma, he borrowed or copied the term "inerrant" (descriptive of the faithful orbital paths of heavenly bodies) from the astronomers and coined the phrase so well known today, "Only the original autographs are inerrant." (Note: Some believe that this statement originated before Warfield's time.)

This sounds good and it is certainly true that the originals were inerrant. But this declaration was a departure from the true fundamentalist belief that had been held before Warfield's time and is held today by many, the writer included. True Bible fundamentalists have believed all along in providentially preserved infallible Hebrew and Greek manuscripts from which the Authorized King James Bible was translated. Of course, no one has a copy of a copy of a copy of the originals. If we have to depend upon the originals, we are all in a bad situation. The originals have not been found.

This brings up an interesting question, why do Westcott-Hort fundamentalist Christians persist in declaring an infallible original and decry preserved inerrant Hebrew and Greek Bible Texts? These same fundamentalists will hold the King James Bible in the air declaring it to be the Word of God and then deny its absolute authority even in its preserved Hebrew and Greek texts.

The writer wonders if these Westcott-Hort fundamentalists accept as reliable, the 90-95% of Bible text that agrees with the Westcott-Hort/Nestle-Aland text, and discard the rest? The writer does not accept a 90-95% preserved text. The Bible would be *obsolete*, if not *absolute*. All of it is providentially preserved or none of it is reliable. The Scriptures are either "all of God" or "not at all." If God only inspired the originals (and He did) and did not preserve them, to whom or to what authority do we anchor our souls? They (or we) have forsaken a preserved Word of God for a phantom original that no one possesses. If God inspired an original perfect Word, why did He lose it?

No one can produce the originals, but the preserved text can be produced. Of what value is original inspiration if the Word of God has not been preserved? Why would an omniscient God inspire an inerrant original for a handful of people only to let it fade away shortly thereafter leaving billions (following generations) in abstract uncertainty?

Did God waste His time in inspiring the originals, being unable to preserve them?

The writer believes that the preservation of the Word of God would be much easier than inspiring the originals. Scholars say that the original manuscripts involved the inspiration and collection of 66 perfectly harmonious books in three languages by about 40 writers of different social, educational, and economic backgrounds over a period of about 1,500 years on three continents. No man will be able to accuse God in the judgment. God preserved all of His Words that He originally inspired.

From a child, Timothy had known the Holy Scriptures (II Timothy 3:15), but it is not likely that Timothy or the early disciples had the *originals*. From this, we can see that God *preserved copies* of the Hebrew and Greek originals.

(**Note:** God did not promise to preserve the original scrolls or the materials upon which the original Words were written, but He did promise to preserve His Words.)

Contrary to what some teach, it was the Scriptures (Words of God) that were inspired, not the writers (2 Timothy 3:16; 2 Peter 1:21; Matthew 4:4).

CHAPTER 6

WHERE IS GOD'S WORD(S) PRESERVED TODAY?

Dr. Ronnie L. Williamson says, "I do believe and defend the KJV as the preserved Word of God for English speaking people today. I do not endorse the New King James, NIV, or the many other translations. These modern versions are based on revised, rediscovered, and rejected texts compiled by a list of 'scholars/higher critics' who were German rationalists, evolutionist who promoted spiritism and racism denying biblical inerrancy. I will stand with the Textus Receptus and the Masoretic Text upon which the KJV is based." *(The Voice in the Wilderness,* August/September 2005, p 4).

Some believe that God preserved His Word somewhere within thousands of manuscripts. The writer believes that God preserved His Word in the ben Chayyim Masoretic Hebrew Text (OT) and the Byzantine Greek Text (NT), not in a maze of over 5,000 texts.

Who is really causing the division?

The writer has heard Westcott-Hort fundamentalist brethren accuse the King James defenders of causing division among the brethren over Bible translations. True fundamentalists have not moved away from the preserved Hebrew and Greek texts of the King James Bible. Who has moved?   Our Westcott-Hort "fundamentalist" brethren moved away. So, who is really causing the division?

Ruckmanites

Ruckmanites: so-called after Peter Ruckman who teaches some extreme views. So, the term, *Ruckmanites,* is a slur intended to discredit those, who not only defend the King James Bible, but also criticize English translations coming from the Westcott-Hort/Nestle'-Aland text that the Westcott-Hort brethren defend.

Sometimes, these Westcott-Hort brethren even get desperate enough to label the King James advocates as *Ruckmanites*. This is another smokescreen for the Westcott-Hort brethren to hide behind. It is common knowledge that traditional Bible fundamentalists do not agree with Peter Ruckman on many of his beliefs.

Wilbur Pickering aptly expressed it this way, "If the Scriptures have not been preserved then the Doctrine of Inspiration is a purely academic matter with no relevance for us today. If we do not have the inspired words or do not know precisely which they be, then the doctrine of Inspiration is inapplicable" *(An Understandable History of the Bible*, P. 21).

David Otis Fuller says, "It ought to be pointed out that those who seem eager to attack the King James and the Greek text behind it, when the enormous difficulties of the Revised Greek Testament are pointed out, will claim the Revised Text is all right because it is like the Greek New Testament from which the King James was translated; on the other hand, when they are not called to account, they will say belittling things about the Received Text and the scholars who translated the King James Bible" (*Which Bible,* p. 246).

The Two Tables of Testimony graven in stone by the hand of God were broken many ways, but The Ten Commandments are with us today. Jehoiakim (king of Judah) penknifed and burned the roll of God's Word, but it is preserved for us today (Jeremiah 36:23, 27-28).

If the reader does not believe the following Scriptures, he is without hope:

Psalms 12:6-7: The Words of the LORD are pure words: as silver tried in a furnace of earth, purified seven times. Thou shalt keep them, O Lord thou shalt preserve them from this generation for ever.

Psalms 119:89: For ever, O LORD, thy Word is settled in heaven.

Isaiah 40:8: The grass withereth, the flower fadeth: but the Word of our God shall stand for ever.

Matthew 24:35: Heaven and earth shall pass away, but my Words shall not pass away.

I Peter 1:25: But the Word of the Lord endureth for ever. And this is the Word which by the Gospel is preached unto you.

Also see Psalms 78:1-8; 105:8; 119:111, 152, 160; Proverbs 22:20-21; Ecclesiastes 3:14; Isaiah 30:8; 59:21; Matthew 4:4; John 12:49-50; 17:8; I Peter 1:23.

Of what value are the originals to anyone if no one possesses them? How could our Lord hold His stewards accountable to His teachings if we do not assuredly have a clearly defined preserved text of His original Words? If we do not have the preserved text, surely God knows!

If we do not have the preserved Words of God, in a single canon, we are at the mercy of the opinions of men.

Psalms 118:8: It is better to trust in the Lord that to put confidence in man.

On page 243 of his excellent book, *The King James Version Defended,* Edward Hills makes a very meaningful and timely statement. He says, "Naturalistic textual criticism regards the special, providential preservation of the Scriptures as of no importance for the study of the New Testament text. But if we concede this, then it follows that the infallible inspiration of the Scriptures is likewise unimportant. For why is it important that God should infallibly inspire the Scriptures, if it is not important that He should preserve them by His special providence?"

Many translators and editors of modern English Bibles will tell you that we cannot have a preserved Bible text

If God did not preserve His Words, to what authority do we appeal? If we do not have an authoritative Bible preserved in one canon (OT and NT) it is reasonable to assume that someone or something else of greater authority is required to instruct us. The critical text theologians claim the privilege of knowing a better text than the one that our King James Bible came from.

Most Of Our English Bibles Came From Only Two Basic Texts:

1) The Masoretic/Byzantine (Majority Text)
2) The Alexandrian/Vaticanus/Sinaiticus/Westcott-Hort/Nestle-Aland revised text that is often referred to as the "Critical Text."

Although it is claimed that the NKJV {New King James Version}, with its 60,000 changes, is based primarily upon the Textus Receptus, it is still a New Age Bible and is not recommended (by reliable scholars) for the sincere reader. The following is copied from *The Defined King James Bible*, p.1681, published by *The Bible For Today Press*, Collingswood, NJ.

Examples in the NKJV:

- "LORD" is thrown out 56 times out of the 6,668.
- "GOD" is ejected 35 times out of the 3,878.
- "JEHOVAH' is altogether missing.
- "Heaven" is missing 48 out of 550 times.
- "Hell" is thrown out 22 out of 54 times.
- "Blood" is deleted 118 out of 375 times.
- "Repent" is ejected 11 out of 43 times.
- "New Testament" is cast out all 6 times.
- "Damnation" is missing all 11 times.

One writer says that NKJV replaced the KJV Hebrew (ben Chayyim) with the corrupt Stuttgart edition (ben Asher) Old Testament.

Some NKJV's (New King James Version) sport the number 666 in the form of a mobius (mo-be-as, ma) on its cover. The most popular New Age magazine "Aquarian

Conspiracy' also has the same symbol. Some claim that the three loops formed are representative of the Trinity.

(**mobius:** a one-side surface constructed from a rectangle by holding one end fixed and rotating the opposite end 180 degrees and applying it to the first end. This symbol is recognized by Luciferians. There is a Mobius Group in Los Angeles which is a leader in investigating psychic phenomena.)

According to Gail Riplinger, The NKJV logo is the ancient symbol for the pagan trinity, not the Christian Trinity. Use of number symbols (like this 666) can be traced back to Pythagoras (582 B.C.), initiate into the Egyptian mysteries. The symbol was popularized again by satanist Aleister Crowley (circa 1900) for the Royal Arch (Lucifer) of the 3rd Degree of the York Order of Masonry. The symbol's shape is duplicated as three initiates join arms and feet, while repeating the names of ancient pagan trinity. The NKJV's symbol can be seen on satanic rock group albums like Led Zeppelin, as well as on New Age bestsellers like the Aquarian Conspiracy.

Knowledge can be a great asset or a great hindrance

The teachers and advocates of Higher Textual Criticism are quick to tell you that they have the superior text and the superior knowledge to translate.

I Corinthians 8:1: "Knowledge puffeth up..."

As one writer stated, "Pride has an astounding effect on the ability of people to receive truth."

Obadiah 3: The pride of thine heart hath deceived thee..."

Knowledge and pride make people very susceptible to deception and error. Irrefutable facts cause those in error to become angry. The shocking thing is that fundamental Bible believing Christian leaders have been duped into following the Westcott-Hort/Nestle-Aland corrupted text. The sad part is that they have led thousands of God's people along with them.

Observe the following Bible cases of deception:

• Innocent Eve was deceived by the serpent (I Timothy 2:14).

• David, a man after God's own heart, was deceived by Ahithophel, his close friend and counselor (II Samuel 16-17).

• Isaac was deceived by his son, Jacob (Genesis 27).

• Jacob was deceived by Leah and her father (Genesis 29).

• Men (both believers and unbelievers) are deceived about the consequences of sin (Galatians 6:7).

• Christians (Arminians or otherwise) who say they have no sin deceive themselves (I John. 1:8).

Certainly, we are neither smarter nor more spiritual than these Bible people. Of course, true believers can be deceived, and some are deceived many times. Scholarship gives no immunity from deception. Actually, many scholars appear to be the easier prey to false manuscripts. The writer has observed that the elitists (well educated) of the fundamentalists appear to be the most susceptible to deception concerning Scriptures. Education can be a tool of great harm as well as a great asset. Actually, most sects and cults were begun by intelligent heretics and well-educated *religionists*.

> *John 16:13a: Howbeit when he, the Spirit of truth, is come, he will guide you into all truth:*

Readers of the NIV will not know if they are reading what God originally caused His Word to say or what the New Age Bible interpreters decided His Word should say.

> *Matthew 15:14: "...And if the blind lead the blind, both shall fall into the ditch."*

The writer has no doubt that some fundamentalist leaders and pastors meant well but trusted the spiritual discernment of uninformed leaders and biased theologians rather than following the leadership of the Holy Spirit.

Gail Riplinger said, "It will be difficult for good honest pastors to swallow their pride and admit that they were wrong."

> *Ephesians 5:1: Be ye therefore followers of God.*

Either this writer is in trouble with God for writing this paper, or fundamentalist leaders (who support New Age Bibles) and moderates (liberals) are in trouble with God for leading His people down the wrong path. Both of us cannot be correct because we are 180 degrees apart. If this writer is wrong, he welcomes the chastisement of God. It is a dangerous thing to tamper with God's Word.

Psalms 138:2: God has magnified His Word above all his name.

Deuteronomy 4:2: Ye shall not add unto the Word which I command you, neither shall ye diminish (take away) ought (any) from it, that ye may keep the commandments of the LORD your God which I command you -

Revelation 22:19: And if any man shall take away from the words of the book of this prophecy, God shall take away his part out of the book of life and out of the holy city, and from the things which are written in this book.

(**Note**: Some believe that Revelation 22:19 only pertains to the book of Revelation and no other Scriptures as Deuteronomy 4:2; 12:32.)

CHAPTER 7

WHAT ABOUT BIBLES IN OTHER LANGUAGES?

The writer is not addressing the translation of the Bible in languages other than English. He is convinced that the King James Bible is an accurately translated English Bible readily available to the masses. The writer believes that God ordained and protected the translation of the King James Bible. The King James Bible did not need to be inspired; it did not need to be inspired because it was accurately AND faithfully translated from the *preserved copies* of the original inspired texts.

Consider the following possibilities concerning God's Word:

• **If** Christ's Words will not pass away, where are they today?

> ***Matthew 24:35: Heaven and earth shall pass away, but my words shall not pass away.***

• **If** the Word is not accurately translated into English, then it is restricted to a few elite Scholars of Hebrew, Aramaic, and Greek.

• **If** God's Word is locked up in ancient languages, then advanced education is absolutely necessary for knowing the Word. Of course, this favors the gifted and the well-educated and practically eliminates the common class of people.

The writer does not believe that God has left the common people to the mercy of biased scholars and shallow theologians.

(Hint: Jesus bypassed the scribes [manuscript scholars of His day] and went to the common people.)

This writer believes that the King James Bible, as translated from the preserved Old Testament Ben Chayyim Hebrew Text and the New Testament Byzantine Greek text, is God's Word for English speaking people.

Major revisions of the 1611 King James Bible?

In order to prop up an argument against the King James Bible, our Westcott-Hort brethren claim that there were four major revisions of the 1611 King James Bible. Other scholars say that these were not major revisions but editions to correct minor spelling errors, typos, etc. Actually, there were more than just a few editions to correct errata of spelling and typos, for even the spelling of words had not been standardized in those days.

Another Westcott-Hort fundamentalist brother's comment:

One Christian editor/writer, who defends some of the English Bible translations from the Westcott-Hort text, carried an article by **Rick Norris** in his newspaper in an apparent attempt to strengthen arguments against those who defend the King James Bible.

"Norris quotes other reliable English Bible translations such as:

1755 translation by John Wesley; the 1833 Bible by Noah Webster; the 1842 Bernard's Bible; the 1850 revision of the KJV New Testament by Baptists Spencer Cone and William Wyckoff; the 1853 English Old Testament by Isaac Leeser; and the 1866 American Bible Union translation based on a 1881 Greek text" (*The Biblical Evangelist,* May/August 1998, p.5).

The writer has no problem with other good English Bible translations. The writer is not familiar with any of these translations and is not aware of their availability. Perhaps these Bibles could be ordered.

The writer is aware of other good English translations in centuries past that were in the line of the Masoretic/Byzantine texts. Where are all of those good modern English Bible translations that our Westcott-Hort brethren recommend?

Norris lauded the following modern Bibles as Bibles coming from the Masoretic and Textus Receptus texts:

NKJV; MKJV; 21th Century KJV; and *Holy Scriptures according to the Masoretic Text; Jay Green's Interlinear Bible; George Ricker Berry's Interlinear Greek New Testament.*

The writer is somewhat familiar with the NKJV, which is not in the writer's opinion a good translation even though it is reported to be a translation mainly of the Traditional Text.

Norris mentioned two Interlinear Bibles of the Masoretic Hebrew and Byzantine Greek that are not considered reading Bibles in the general sense. This writer has both Interlinear Bibles of George Ricker Berry and Jay P. Green, Sr. These self-translating Bibles are geared for students of the Bible. Most Christians are not familiar with them.

It seems strange to this writer that many Westcott-Hort fundamentalists, who profess to love the Lord and His Word, are quick to point out and attack any small *seeming* error of translation in the King James Bible.

Bibles in the King James line

Some earlier Bible versions in the Textus Receptus (King James) line are:

The Gothic Version (4th century); Chrysostom's (500 AD); Daniel Bomberg's Hebrew Edition (1516-1517); Ben Chayyim Masoretic Text (1906, 1912); The Old Peshitta; The Old Latin; Erasmus Greek N.T. (1516); The Complutensian Polyglot (1522); Martin Luther's German Bible (1522); William Tyndale's Bible (1525); The French Version of Oliveton (1535); The Coverdale Bible (1535); The Matthews Bible (1537); The Taverners Bible (1539); The Great Bible (1539-41); The Stephanus Greek NT (1546-51); The Geneva Bible (1557-60); The Bishops' Bible (1568); The Spanish Version (1569); The Beza Greek NT (1598); The Czech Version (1602); and The Italian Version of Diodati (1607).

(Beza's 5th Edition of 1598 is the Greek text from which our AV [Authorized Version] Bible came from, *Fundamentalist Distortions on Bible Versions*, p. 33.)

Earlier churches that used the Received Text of the King James Bible:

All of the Apostolic Churches; the churches in Palestine; the Syrian Church at Antioch; the Italic Church in Northern Italy (157 AD); the Gallic Church of Southern France (177 AD); the Celtic Church in Great Britain; the Church of Scotland and Ireland; the Pre-Waldensian churches; the Waldensians (120 AD); the Greek Orthodox Church (earlier and now); and the churches of the Reformation.

Some of the modern English Bibles other than the NIV:

Other New Age versions include: NASB; NEB; REB; LB; JB; NJB; ASV; RSV; KJ21; CEV; NRSV; TEV; NCV; Phillips; New Jerusalem; New Living; the Interpreters Bible; NAB; KJ21 (21st Century KJV).

- The basic Hebrew and Greek texts of most of these modern Bibles are from the same Hebrew and Greek texts of the Roman Catholic Bible and the Jehovah Witness New World Translation Bible.

- The King James is a trustworthy English translation of the Word of God. It is God's Word in English. The NIV and other New Age versions only *contain* the Word of God.

- A Bible translation is very important. Since very few people know Hebrew and Greek, we are dependent upon an accurate translation from preserved copies of the preserved texts.

- Even if the New Age Bibles were accurately translated from their Hebrew and Greek sources, they are still a product of corrupt manuscripts that differ from the Traditional Text in thousands of places.

Observe that NIV editors consulted "more important early versions" where the Masoretic text seemed doubtful (*NIV Women's Devotional Bible*, p. XI of the preface).

"A little leaven leaveneth the whole lump" (Galatians 5:9; I Corinthians 5:6).

One writer says, "The emerging new Christianity -- with its substitution of riches for righteousness, a crown for a cross, and an imitation for a new creation -- is shown to be a direct result of the wording in new versions."

Who are some of the contributors to the corruption of the Bible Texts?

A list of all would be impossible. Following are some of them:

- Apostate scribes from every century
- "Colwell (late President of the University of Chicago) found that as early as AD 200 scribes were altering manuscripts, changing them from a Majority-type text to a minority type" (*New Age Bible Versions*, p. 484).
- Marcion, a Gnostic (120-160 AD). Irenaeus named Marcion "the heretic"; Justin Martyr, Tertullian, and Irenaeus referred to him as, "The beast"
- Origen (185-251 AD) Taught preexistence of souls (reincarnation); taught universalism; taught purgatory
- Essenes (2nd century) Rejected Christ as Lord.
- Clement of Alexander, Egypt. Student of Philo and Pantaneus and mentor of Origen

- Arius. Taught that Jesus was a created being not externally generated
- Taitan. Constructed his Diatessaron in which he attempted to weave the four-fold
narratives of the gospels into one (*Foes of The King James Bible*, p. 76).
- Saturninus (120 AD). He and his followers taught that marriage was a production of Hell. They opposed gospel teaching on marriage.
- Basilides (about 134 AD). He and his followers invented a gospel of their own, a gospel of Basilides (*Foes of the Kings James Bible*, p. 77)
- Valentinus (about 140 AD). He and his followers (Ebionites) interpolated and otherwise perverted one of the four gospels until it suited their own purposes (*Foes of The King James Bible*, p. 77).
- Heracleon. Was deliberately censured by Origen for having corrupted the text of the fourth gospel in many places. Even Origen, the heretic, said that Heracleon, the heretic, must be censured for having corrupted the text of John (*Foes of The King James Bible*, p.77).
- Theodotus (about 192 AD). Was a Gnostic who used a depraved copy of John chapter 1 verse 3 (*Foes of The King James Bible*, p.77).
- Manes (about 261 AD). Wrote his own fabricated heretical gospel (*Foes of The King James Bible,* p. 77).
- Eusebius. Prepared Codex Aleph (book form of Sinaiticus manuscript) and Codes B (book form of Vaticanus manuscript).

• Tischendorf. Instrumental in introducing Sinaiticus and Vaticanus texts.

• J.J. Griesbach (1745-1812). His 1796 edition of the Greek text removed the ending of Mark 16 (vv. 9-20). (*Way of Life Enc. of the Bible & Christianity*, p.55); openly denied the Deity of Christ.

• Karl Lachmann (1793-1851). Discarded the readings of Received Text in favor of what he considered the oldest and best text represented in the Vaticanus and a few other similarly corrupt manuscripts (*Way of Life Enc. of the Bible & Christianity*, p.55).

• Samuel Tregelles (1813-1875). Same view as Lachmann. Tregelles lauded Lachmann for casting aside the so-called Textus Receptus and accepted the Vaticanus as actual authority (*Way of Life Enc. of the Bible & Christianity*, p.55).

• Henry Thayer. Denied the deity of Christ

• Philip Schaff (Chairman of the ASV of 1901). Said that none of the variant readings affect Doctrine (*Defending the King James Bible*, p. 131); a transcendentalist.

• J.B. Phillips. Practiced necromancy (communication with the dead).

• B.B. Warfield. Promoted "inerrant originals" thus downplaying "providential preservation."

• Samuel Taylor Coleridge (English poet). Unitarian who considered only parts of the Bible inspired; spoke of the virgin birth as "an excrescence" (from "execrate,"

something detestable) of faith, which should be discarded"; said that human reason rather than

Scriptures was the foundation of Christian belief (*Tabernacle Essays on Bible Translation*, pp.12, 14).

• A.T. Pierson. "It is remarkable how faithful all the standard translations are...not one doubtful disputed rendering affects a single vital doctrine of the Word of God." *Defending The King James Bible*, p. 132).

• Charles Hodge. Felt that theistic evolution acceptable under certain conditions; first to take up German naturalistic text criticism (*Tabernacle Essays on Bible Translation*, p. 43).

• Robert L. Sumner. "*...the rare parts about which there is still uncertainty do not effect in any way any doctrine.*" (*Defending the King James Bible*, p.133).

• G. Vance Smith. (A Unitarian who assisted Westcott-Hort in the 1881 revision).

• C. D. Brokenshire. Trained at Princeton during Warfield's tenure (early 1900's) and helped propagate revised text through his influence in fundamentalist schools.

• Bible rationalists (especially 19th century German critics)

(**Note:** This writer is not implying that these men were not saved or did not love the Lord. The writer is neither capable nor worthy of judging the motives of men's' hearts. However, the wheat can be influenced by tares, which grow together with the wheat, in the kingdom of heaven (Matthew 13:25-30).

CHAPTER 8

WHO IS ACCOUNTABLE?

The list above is far from complete. Even fundamentalist leaders (who promote poor translations) and Christians who knowingly or unknowingly buy and use the New Age English Bibles are accountable. The writer has not, to date, met a user of the NIV who has searched out the origin of its source (perhaps some have and are satisfied). The attitude of most Church members appears to be "If it is good enough for my pastor, it is good enough for me."

Lester Roloff said, "The Bible does not need to be re-written; it needs to be re-read."

What are some of the corrupt texts?

- Alexandrinus Manuscript
- Vaticanus Manuscript
- Sinaiticus Manuscript
- The Latin Vulgate
- The Biblia Hebraica of Kittel or Stuttgartensia
- Ben Asher Hebrew Text
- The Samaritan Pentateuch
- Westcott/Hort (Revised Text of 1881)
- Nestle/Aland (about 27 editions)
- The Dead Sea Scrolls (believed to be a product of the Essene cult who rejected Christ as Lord). Some say that parts of the Dead Sea Scrolls are exactly like the KJV Hebrew text.

2 Corinthians 2:17: For we are not as many which corrupt the Word of God..."

Revelation 22:19: And if any man shall take away from the words of the book of this prophecy, God shall take away his part out of the book of life, and out of the holy city, and from the things which are written in this book

Dean Burgon says: "The impurity of the texts exhibited by Codices B (Vaticanus) and Aleph (Sinaiticus) is not a matter of opinion, but a matter of fact. These are two of the least trustworthy documents in existence.... Codices B and Aleph are, demonstrably, nothing else but specimens of the depraved class thus characterized" *(Which Bible?* p. 307).

Dean John Burgon

(**Note:** the writer readily concedes that **Dean John Burgon** was not correct in all of his biblical analyses. Example: According to *The Biblical Evangelist* dated January-February, 2008, p. 4, in his reply to Bishop Ellicott, Burgon scoffed at the idea that there was any perfect Greek text (apart from the original autographs, of course), suggesting that one would be insane to make such a claim. He said, "But pray, who in his senses, -what sane man in Great Britain, -ever dreamed of regarding the 'received," – aye, or any other known 'text,' as 'a standard from which there shall be no appeal'? "Have I ever done so? Have I ever implied as much? If I have, show me where (according to the editor of The Biblical Evangelist, Robert Sumner).

Of course, the writer believes the God's Word is preserved for us in the Old Testament Ben Chayyim Hebrew

Text and the New Testament Byzantine Greek text (Isaiah 40:8; Psalms12:6-7; 138:2; Jeremiah 36:23, 27-28; I Peter 1:24-25; Matthew 24:35).

If the exact text in not preserved, where should we look? How could anyone be held accountable to God if we do not have inerrant manuscripts of Hebrew and Greek?

Is it good (well) enough that God's Word is contained in the New Age Bibles?

David Cloud

David Cloud says, "You can show someone the Gospel of the grace of Christ even with a Roman Catholic version. You can prove the deity or Christ even with the perverted New World Translation used by the Jehovah's Witnesses. You can teach the doctrine of the Atonement even from a perversion such as the Today's English Bible, which deletes the word "blood" in most major passages. This shows the marvelous hand of God to confound the efforts of the devil. But this does not mean that the changes made in these and other new translations are not significant" *(The Encyclopedia of the Bible and Christianity*, p. 61).

The writer agrees with Mr. Cloud.

All of the New English Versions have one thing in common with each other: All are against the King James Bible:

They all claim to be superior to the Authorized King James Bible. They never claim to be an improvement over each other - RSV, ASV, NASV, NIV, LB, etc. Isn't it strange that no one ever strives to make a Bible version clearer and more accurate than any other New Age English

Bible? They are always making a Bible better than the King James? A phony makes itself conspicuous by its claim of being superior to the authentic.

To this writer, it seems *strange* that Roman Catholic scholars, apostate Protestants, and Westcott-Hort fundamentalists all agree on criticizing the King James Bible.

Dr. Gordon D. Fee

Dr. Gordon D. Fee (professor at Wheaton College), said, "The contemporary translations as a group have one thing in common: they tend to agree against the King James Version...in omitting hundreds of words, phrases, and verses" (Barry Burton, *Let's Weight the Evidence)*.

New Age Bibles are called "translations"

It also seems strange to the writer that most of the New Age Bibles are called "translations" and the King James Bible is called a "version." The writer believes that the opposite is true.

Another writer said, "New versions are sweeping the church like an uncontrolled brush fire."

The key men instrumental in the production of another New Age Bible

Although this writing is concerned mainly with the NIV, **the words** of one of the key men instrumental in the production of another New Age Bible is noteworthy:

"I must under God renounce every attachment
to the New American Standard...I'm afraid I'm in
trouble with the Lord...We laid the groundwork; I wrote

the format; I helped interview some of the translators; I sat with the translator; I wrote the preface...

I'm in trouble; I can't refute these arguments; it's wrong, it's terribly wrong; it's frighteningly wrong; and what am I going to do about it? I can no longer ignore these criticisms I am hearing and I can't refute them...

When questions began to reach me at first I was quite offended. However, in attempting to answer, I began to sense that something was not right about the NASV. Upon investigation, I wrote my very dear friend, Mr. Lockman, explaining that I was forced to renounce all attachment to the **NASV**...The product is grievous to my heart and helps to complicate matters in these already troublous times...The deletions are absolutely frightening...there are so many...Are we so naive that we do not suspect Satanic deception in all of this? I don't want anything to do with it...

The finest leaders that we have today...haven't gone into it {the new version's use of a corrupted Greek text}, just as I hadn't gone into it...That's how easily one can be deceived...I'm going to talk to him {Dr. George Sweeting, then president of Moody Bible Institute} about these things...

You can say the **Authorized Version {KJV}** is absolutely correct. How correct? 100% correct! If you must stand against everyone else, stand." *(Dr. Frank Logsdon, Which Bible is God's Word, p. 49).*

(Dr. S. Franklin Logsdon is a former pastor of Moody Memorial Church and was a member of the Amplified Version committee.)

Christian bookstore with books unfavorable to the KJV

In a recent visit to a fundamentalist university bookstore in Greenville, SC, David Cloud said, "I was interested to see how many volumes were available to tear down the King James Bible and its underlying Greek Text, and that attacks it defenders. There were at least ten books in this category..." Brother Cloud went on to say that the university claims to love the KJV and boasts that it is the only Bible used in their chapel and public meetings. Brother Cloud said, 'Yet in the *preachers boys* classes they tear it apart and say that the best bible is the NASV. Why would you use what you believe to be an inferior Bible in public meetings? Maybe you don't think that is hypocrisy, but I do'" (*The Perilous Times*, p. 7, MAY/JUNE, 2006).

The NASV was wrong

Dr. Frank Logsdon, who was on the committee that produced the NASV, said that the NASV was wrong, very wrong. Dr. Logsdon also added that the KJV was very right (Dr. Frank Logsdon, *Which Bible is God's Word*, p. 49).

Other disclaimers of the Westcott-Hort Text

Dr. Alfred Martin (past vice-president of Moody Bible Institute) does not appear to be a fan of the NIV or NASB.

Dr. Martin said, "The theories and Greek text behind the new versions collapse when subject to close scrutiny" *(Which Bible is God's Word*, p. 49).

Dr. Martin also says, "Many people, even today, who have no idea what the Westcott-Hort theory is...accept the labors of those two scholars without question...an amusing and amazing spectacle presents itself: many of the textbooks, books of bible interpretation, innumerable secondary works go on repeating the Westcott and Hort dicta although the foundations have been seriously shaken, even in the opinion of former Hortians" *(New Age Bible Versions*, p. 400).

The brilliant lawyer, Sir Robert Anderson, famed head of Scotland Yard, said about the changes of the Westcott-Hort text, "The Revisers' changes in the text are new errors, and not the correction of old errors" *(Which Bible?* p.122).

Anything but THAT one! (David W. Daniels, *Battle Cry*, p. 5, Jan/Feb 2006)

Find ANOTHER PUBLISHER.

Lately I have spoken to two different Christian authors. Each has told me a similar story. He wanted to reprint his book, but with a different Bible version. Here is basically how the conversation went.

"I would like to issue the next edition of my book using a different Bible version."

"That's fine. What did you have in mind?"

"Well, first I have a few questions. If I wanted to change the version to the NIV, would you print my book?"

"Of course."

"What if I wanted to use the NLT (New Living Translation). Would that be OK?"

"Why not?"

"Is the NKJV (New King James Version) alright with you?"

"We'd be happy to."

"How about the Message Bible?"

"No problem."

"Then I'd like to change it to the King James Bible."

"I'm sorry. You need to find ANOTHER PUBLISHER."

What they found was this. It doesn't matter what Bible they want to use, as long as it isn't a King James Bible. They can pick a Bible that takes away words, even whole verses. They can pick a paraphrase that makes the Bible say all sorts of things it was never meant to say. They can pick a Bible that is soft on the sin of homosexuality, changes verse about the deity of Christ, hides the fact that God promises to preserve His words, and sneaks Roman Catholic doctrine in while no one is looking. They can even use multiple different versions that totally disagree with one another. But as soon as they want to use the King James Bible, the doors close in their faces.

You know, you can tell a lot more about a book by its enemies that by its cover.

I must tell you: both authors did find someone else to publish their books using the King James. God is always faithful.

The writer of this paper is not the least bit surprised! Actually, the surprise would be if worldly book publishers catered to the King James Bible in these last days of apostasy.

CHAPTER 9

COPYRIGHT VERSUS NON-COPYRIGHT

Of course, the NIV is bound by a copyright just as are all the other Modern English versions. The authors and publishers receive a royalty on the sales. This is not true for the King James Bible. God has preserved and protected the text of the King James Bible, and no one can copyright it. Neither is our God the author of confusion (I Corinthians 14:33).

(**Note**: The very text of the King James Bible itself cannot be copyrighted. However, many Reference Bibles using the Hebrew and Greek text of the King James can be copyrighted because they use their own prescribed annotations, system of references, footnotes, etc.)

Scriptural salvation denied by NIV editor

The NIV's chief editor vaunts his version's heresy saying: "This [his own translation] shows the great error that is so prevalent today in some orthodox Protestant circles, namely the error that regeneration depends upon faith and that in order to be born again man must first accept Jesus as Savior" (Edwin Palmer, *The Holy Spirit*, p. 83, Baker Book House, 1974, Grand Rapids, Michigan").

If the NIV editors and any others do not believe John 3:3; Acts 4:12; Romans 4:4-6; 5:15; 6:23; Galatians

2:16; Ephesians 2:8, 9, Titus 3:5, and Acts 16:31, they are aliens to the grace of God.

Why so many new Bible versions?

From 1380 until 1991, 135 whole English Bibles and 293 English New Testaments have been published, a total of 428 new Bibles.

(These Bibles are listed in D.A. Waite's, *Defending the King James Bible*, pp. 198-212.)

Logical questions Arise: Why so many translations or versions? What is the motive?

The writer is convinced that the answer is mainly twofold:

1.) Printing new Bibles has become big business. There is nothing wrong with making a profit from printing Bibles when profit is not the main reason or only motive. The New Age versions are copyrighted and bring in millions of dollars to the publishers and translators through sales and royalties.

> *"For the love of money is the root of all evil:..." (I Timothy 6:10).*

(Neither did the moneychangers in the temple care about the holy things of God: Matthew 21:12-13; Mark 11:15-16.)

The writer believes what God's Word says concerning false religionists.

> *"For they that are such serve not our Lord Jesus Christ, but their own belly; and by good words and fair speeches deceive the hearts of the simple" (Romans 16:18)*

2.) Next, after the filthy lucre motive, the second reason for so many new Bibles is that Satan seeks to deceive the world by counterfeiting God's Word. He is subtly supplanting God's Word and forming his own global bible with very little resistance in the realm of Christendom. Satan can tolerate a form of religion but hates the power thereof. His religion is a clever copy of Christ's religion. He knows that his days are numbered and desires to damn as many souls as possible before his brief earthly reign is over (Ephesians 2:2; I Peter 5:8; 2 Corinthians 4:4; Revelation 12:12).

(Satan knows a lot about the Bible; remember he cleverly misquoted God's Word in the garden of Eden and misapplied Scriptures when tempting Jesus in the wilderness.)

Satan's two earth henchmen (beast out of the sea [the antichrist]; beast out of the earth [the false prophet]) are listed in Revelation 13 where his one-world religion (Babylon, Mother of Harlots) is in view. This religious whore's description and destruction are given in Revelation Chapters 17, 18. Remember that this religious harlot of the book of Revelation will have her own international bible version, and you can be sure that it will not be a product of the preserved Hebrew and Greek text of the King James Bible.

> *Proverbs 30:12: There is a generation that are pure in their own eyes, and yet is not washed from their filthiness.*

Arrogant teachers and professors

Many times, some fundamentalists sound just like liberals when teaching the Word of God. They love to exhibit their spiritual prowess and Greek knowledge when expounding

Scriptures texts.

Their textual expositions go something like this:

- "A better translation would be..."
- "A more accurate rendering is..."
- "The King James mistranslated here, it should be..."
- "This must be a copyist's error..."

In some cases, these statements may be true to a small degree (some English words have changed their meaning since 1611 and it is difficult to translate word-perfect from one language to another), but then the so-called Bible expositor will go on to give a one-sided view of his choosing (or of his literature). Of course, there is nothing wrong with textual exposition and exploring various shades of word meanings, that's just teaching. Even personal opinions may be all right in obscure passages if the teacher makes sure that his students know that it is just speculation on his part. But this writer is sure that some have gone so far as to correct God's Word.

Even the beginner Bible student knows that most Hebrew and Greek words are translated into a variety of English Words.

Examples of various shades of meanings of Greek words:

• *Diakonos* is translated into 3 English words: deacon; minister; servant.

• *Anothen* is translated into 5 English words: above; again; anew; first; top. (This is the word Jesus used to tell Nicodemus that he must be born again, John 3:7.)

• *Diakonia* is translated into 9 English words: administration; minister; ministration; ministering; ministry; office; relief; service; serving.

• *Didomi* is translated into about 22 English words: add; adventure; bestow; cause; commit; deliver; give; grant; make; minister; offer; power; put; receive; render; set; shew; smite; suffer; take; utter; yield.

• *Logos* is translated into about 25 English words: account; cause; communication; do; doctrine; fame; intent; matter; mouth; preaching; question; reason; reckon; report; rumour; saying; show; speech; talk; thing; tidings; treatise; utterance; word; work.

• *Poieo* is translated into about 31 English words or word forms: abide; appoint; bear; bring; cause; commit; continue; deal with; do; execute; exercise; fulfill; gain; give; hold; keep; make; mean; observe; ordain; perform; provide; purpose; put; shew; shoot forth; spend; take; tarry; work; yield.

• *Ginomai* is translated into about 39 English words or word forms: arise; assemble; become; befall; behave; bring; come; continue; divide; do; end; fall; far; finish; follow; forbid; grow; have; keep; marry; means (by...of); ordain; pass; past; perform; place (take); prefer; prove; publish; shew; sound; spent; spring; take; turn; use; was etc.; wax; work.

> English *master:* 6 Greek words
> English *judgment:* 8 Greek words
> English *but:* 12 Greek words
> English *by:* 11 Greek words
> English *for:* 18 Greek words
> English *in:* 15 Greek words
> English *of:* 13 Greek words
> English *on:* 9 Greek words

Some Greek words, such as *aima* (haima), can only be translated into one English word, blood, not death as some modern English versions translate (*Good News Bible,* for example).

From these few examples, we can easily see that it is not always possible to translate every word, exactly word for word, from one language to another. Pseudo-scribes greatly compound translation difficulties and arrogate themselves as judges of God's Word. Of course, these New Age scribes commonly militate against the King James Traditional Text.

As mentioned earlier in this writing, the writer has observed a definite trend in Christendom: the well-educated tend to be the most susceptible to deception by New Age Bibles. The writer is thankful to God for the well-educated who are not deceived by New Age Bibles. Some are quoted in this writing.

A sexless NIV

NIV has now published a new version called The Holy Bible-New International Version Inclusive Language Edition" or NI-VILE. The publisher of this gender-neutral version, which strives to discount sexual gender, is Hodder & Stoughton of England. The New Testament was completed in 1995, and the entire Bible was ready for distribution in 1996. In June 1997, the Southern Baptists were instrumental in dissuading the publication of this gender-neutral version in America. They were pleased with the "old" NIV version.

An article in the *World Magazine* (March 29, 1997) also contributed to the dissuasion of the gender-neutral translation (Lecture of Dr. Dell Johnson, *The Leaven in Fundamentalism*, Copyright 1998 Pensacola Christian College).

Dr. DA Waite says, "Dr. Kenneth Barker, the Chairman of the 15 member Committee for Biblical Translation (CBT), stated in Greenville, South Carolina, a few years ago, that the NIV was committed to revising its work every 10 years, and that the work on its 2000 A.D. edition was already in progress. He did not mention, however, that this CBT was pushing for this gender-neutral edition for the year 2000"--(B.F.T. #2768, *A Brief Analysis of the NIV INCLLUSIVE LANGUAGE EDITION*, p. 4).

CHAPTER 10

WHO SHOULD CHRISTIANS LISTEN TO?

As a warning to the reader, some fundamentalist schools that previously stood with the KJV Bible have since weakened their position and become very tolerant toward New Age Bible Versions (even since this paper was first written in the 1990's). The writer believes that this compromise is another significant end-time characteristic of the age of apostasy and the drawing near of the translation of the Church (I Corinthians 15:51-58; Titus 2:13; I Thessalonians 4:13-18).

Christians tend to listen to one of three sources:

1.) Unbelieving spiritualists and scribes who corrupt the Scriptures by deleting, adding, and changing.

2.) Believers who are either,

    (a.) Biased

    (b.) Misinformed

    (c.) Uninformed

    (d.) Carnal and walk as men

    (e.) Deceived

3.) Believers who are informed and led of God's Holy Spirit (John 16:13; 2 Timothy 2:15).

(True fundamentalists hold to God's preserved Words.)

In reference to the controversy over whether or not God has preserved His Word today, "If we do not have an infallible, inerrant Bible today, what else really matters? Let us eat, drink, and be merry."

> *Psalms 11:1: If the foundations be destroyed, what can the righteous do?*

If the reader has read this far and believes that God's Word is preserved for us today, he is absolutely obligated to investigate the NIV matter as well as other modern Bible translations to see if these things be so (Acts 17:11; John 5:39; II Timothy 2:15; I John 4:6; Romans 14:12).

> *Amos 8:11: Behold, the days come, saith the Lord GOD, that I will send a famine in the land, not a famine of bread, nor a thirst for water, but of hearing the Words of the Lord.*

ABOUT THE AUTHOR

The writer was born in Greenville, SC in 1934 and was a lifetime resident except for two years in the US Army (Fort Jackson, S.C. and Fort Carson, Colorado) and two years residence in Florida.

After separation (honorably) from the US Army, the writer returned to Greenville, SC and married at age 27 to Christine Moore, an old acquaintance from an adjacent neighborhood. The Lord blessed us with six daughters, Debbie, Donna, Dale, Denise, Deree, and Dena.

A short time after marriage, the writer was convicted of his lost condition as a sinner and after a miserable time under conviction the writer confessed his sin and lost condition to God and was saved.

The writer was 40 years of age when he began attending college (3 years, no diploma).

The writer retired as a chemical technologist from Morton International Chemical Company in 1996. Before retirement, the writer had the urge to write on Bible subjects and wished that he had more time to study. Upon retirement, the writer bought a computer and became a novice writer.

The writer now resides in Easley, S.C.

D. Helton has written several documents and books, as well as the books or booklets: "Jesus is God," "Evolution, Another False Religion of Humanism," "Cremation: Christian or Pagan," "Is The Gap Theory Credible?" "Does Water

Baptism Save," "Can a Saved Person Become Unsaved," and several others, available here:

http://www.theoldpathspublications.com/Pages/Authors/Helton.htm#God

Dennis Helton
200 Home Place Drive
Easley, SC 29640

John 5:24 Verily, verily, I say unto you, He that heareth my word, and believeth on him that sent me, hath everlasting life, and shall not come into condemnation; but is passed from death unto life.

BIBLIOGRAPHY:

American Dictionary of the English Language--Noah Webster 1828, Foundation For

American Christian Education, San Francisco, California

Authorized King James Version, Oxford University Press.

Berry, George Ricker *The Classic Greek Dictionary, fourteenth printing*, Copyright 1927, Follett Publishing Company -- New York; Chicago, 1956; Los Angeles.

Berry, George Ricker *The Interlinear Literal Translation of the Greek New Testament*,

Zondervan Publishing House, Grand Rapids, Michigan.

Bratcher, Robert G. *Why So Many Bibles*, American Bible Society, 450 Park Avenue, New York 22, New York.

Burgon, John William *A Brief Summary of The Causes of the Corruption of the Traditional Text*, Edited by Edward Miller/Summarized by DA Waite, The Bible For Today Press, 900 Park Avenue, Collingswood, NJ 08108.

Burton, Barry *Let's Weigh the Evidence*, Chick Publications, P.O. Box 662, Chino, CA 91708-0662.

Carter, Dr. Mickey P. *Things That Are Different Are Not The Same*, Landmark Baptist Press, 2222 East Hinson Avenue, Haines City, Florida 33844-4902.

Carson, D. A. *The King James Version Debate*, Baker Books, P.O. Box 6287, Grand Rapids, MI   49516-6287

Cimino, Rev. Dick *The Book*, Wonderful Word Publishers, Inc., 107 W. Lincoln, P.O.   Box   2583, Harlingen, Texas 78550.

Cloud, David W. *Way of Life Encyclopedia of the Bible and Christianity*, Way of Life Literature, 1219 North Harns Road, Oak Harbor, Washington 98277.

Concise Bible Dictionary, Believers Bookshelf, Inc., CANADA-USA.

Contemporary English Version American Bible Society, New York, Copyright 1995

Custer, Stewart *The Truth About The King James Version Controversy*,   Bob Jones University Press, Greenville, SC 29614.

Englishman's Greek Concordance of the New Testament, Ninth Edition, London: Samuel Bagster and Sons (Limited), 80, Wigmore Street, W.1.

Fuller, David Otis *Which Bible?*, Grand Rapids International Publications, Copyright 1970, 1972, 1975.

Gipp, Dr. Samuel C. *An Understandable History of the Bible*, Copyright 1987 Samuel C. Gipp, Bible Believers Baptist Bookstore, 1252 Aurora Road, Macedonia, Ohio 44056.

Gipp, Dr. Samuel C. *The Answer Book*, Bible & Literature Missionary Foundation, 713 Cannon Boulevard, Shelbyville, TN 37160.

Grady, Dr. William P. *Final Authority*, Grady Publications, Inc., Copyright 1993, P.O. Box 5217, Knoxville, Tennessee 37928

Green, Jay P. Sr. *The Interlinear Hebrew-Aramaic Old Testament*, The Trinitarian Bible Society, London, England.

Hills, Edward F. *The King James Version Defended*, Copyright© 1984 by Marjorie J. Hills, The Christian Research Press, PO. Box 13023, Des Moines, Iowa 50310-0023

Hislop, Alexander *The Two Babylons*, Loizeaux Brothers, Neptune, New Jersey.

Living Bible Tyndale House Publishers, Wheaton, Illinois, Copyright 1971

New American Standard Bible The Foundation Press Publications, Box 277, La Habra, Calif. 90631

Nettleton, David *Our Infallible Bible*, Regular Baptist Press, 1300 North Meacham Road, P.O. Box 95500, Schaumburg, Illinois 60195.

New Combined Bible Dictionary and Concordance, The Baker Book House, Grand Rapids, Michigan.

New English Bible Oxford University Press, Cambridge University Press, 1961

New International Version (Women's Devotional Bible), Copyright 1990 by the Zondervan Corp.

New International Version, Copyright NY Bible Soc. Internet 1973.

New Jerusalem Bible, The Doubleday, 666 Fifth Avenue, New York, New York 10103

New King James Version, Thomas Nelson Publishers, 1982.

New World Translation of the Holy Scriptures, Watch Tower Bible & Tract Society of New York, Inc., Copyright 1961.

Nicholas, David R. *Foundations of Biblical Inerrancy*, BMH Books, P.O. Box 544, Winona Lake, Indiana 46590.

Pettingill, William L. *Bible Questions Answered*, Zondervan Publishing House, Grand Rapids, Michigan.

Pickering, Ernest *Questions and Answers About Bible Translations*, Baptist World Mission, P.O. Box 1463, Decatur, AL 35602.

Revised Standard Version The World Publishing Company, 2231 West 110th Street, Cleveland 2, Ohio, Copyright 1962

Rice, John R. *Our God-Breathed Book The Bible*, Sword Of The Lord Publishers, P.O. Box 1099, Murfreesboro, TN.

Riplinger, Gail *Which Bible is God's Word*, Hearthstone Publishing, Ltd., 500 Beacon Dr., Oklahoma City, OK 73127.

Riplinger, Gail *New Age Bible Versions*, A.V. Publications Corp., P.O. Box 280, Ararat, VA 24053.

Riplinger, Gail *The Language of the King James Bible*, AV Publications Corp., PO Box 280, Ararat, VA 24053

Sabiers, Karl G. *How The Bible Came Down Through The Centuries*, Robertson Publishing Company, 593 Glendale Boulevard, Los Angeles, California.

Salliby, Chick *If the Foundations Be Destroyed*, Word and Prayer Ministries, P.O. Box 361, Fiskdale, MA 01518-0361.

Sightler, James H., M.D.*A Testimony Founded For Ever,* Second Edition (The King James Bible Defended in Faith and History), Sightler Publications, 25 Sweetbriar Road, Suite 1-A, Greenville, SC 29615

Sightler, James H., M.D. *Silver Words and Pure*, Sightler Publications, 25 Sweetbriar Road, Suite 1-A, Greenville, SC 29615

Sightler, James H, M.D. *Tabernacle Essays on Bible Translation*, Copyright 1993 by Tabernacle Baptist Church, Greenville, SC 29611.

Sightler, James H., M.D. Westcott's New Bibles, Sightler Publications, 25 Sweetbriar Road, Suite 1-A, Greenville, SC 29615

Smith's Bible Dictionary, Barbour and Company, Inc., 164 Mill Street, Westwood, New Jersey 07675

Strong, James *Strong's Exhaustive Concordance Of The Bible*, Abingdon Press, New York - Nashville.

Tenney, Merrill C. *The Zondervan Pictorial Bible Dictionary*, Zondervan Publishing House, Grand Rapids, Michigan 49530.

The New Testament In Modern English - By J.B. Phillips, The MacMillan Co., NY 1962

Todays English Version/Good News For Modern Man American Bible Society 1966, NY

Unger, Merrill F. *Ungers Bible Dictionary*, Moody Press, Chicago, Illinois 60610, Copyright 1957 by The Moody Bible Institute of Chicago.

Young, Robert *Young's Analytical Concordance to the Bible, 22nd American Edition*, Wm. B. Eerdmans Publishing Company, Grand Rapids, Michigan.

Websters Ninth New Collegiate Dictionary Merriam-Webster Inc., Publishers, Springfield, Massachusetts, U.S.A..

Waite, D. A. *Four Reasons For Defending The King James Bible*, The Bible For Today, 900 Park Avenue, Collingswood, N.J. 08108.

Waite, Dr. D. A. *Defending the King James Version*, The Bible For Today Press, 900 Park Avenue, Collingswood, N.J. 08108.

Waite, Rev. D.A. *The New International Version*, The Bible For Today, #1749-P, 900 Park Avenue, Collingswood, N. J. 08108.

Waite, D.A. *NIV Inclusive Edition NI-VILE*, B.F.T. #2768. Copyright 1997, 900 Park Avenue, Collingswood, N.J. 08108.

Waite, D.A. Fundamentalist Distortions on Bible Versions, The Bible For Today Press, 900 Park Avenue, Collingswood, N.J. 08108

Waite, D.A. *A Brief Summary of The Causes of the Corruption of the Traditional Text*, By Dean John William Burgon, Edited by Edward Miller-1896, Summarized by D.A. Waite, The Bible for Today, 900 Park Avenue, Collingswood, NJ 08108

Waite, D.A. *Foes of the King James Bible Refuted*, The Bible For Today Press, 900 Park Avenue, Collingswood, N.J. 08108

Whiston, William *Josephus - Complete Works*, Kreel Publications, Grand Rapids, Michigan 49501.

World Book Encyclopedia, The World Book-Childcraft International, Inc., Copyright 1980, U.S.A.